Hidden
ENGLAND

ELLIE WALKER-ARNOTT

INTRODUCTION

This book invites you to approach England differently, to step away from the well-trodden tourist track, swerve the coach trippers and explore the country's more secretive sights. It helps you look beyond the obvious and seek out the understated, unexpected and unusual.

The locations in this book have been picked either because they're not very well known or because they provide an element of surprise when you stumble across them. You'll find everything from an underground grotto plastered in seashells and an open-air theatre clinging to a Cornish clifftop to a perfectly spherical treehouse and a cloud-watching station surrounded by sand dunes.

Some of the places featured evoke a strong sense of the past or something otherworldly you can't quite pin down, while others are innovative and brand-new. You'll come across things that aren't usually associated with England, like surfing lakes, wild bison and vineyards. A few might be places you've heard of or even visited before (what's hidden to some is obvious to those who live right next door) while others are half-forgotten, hard to reach, hidden in plain sight or basically invisible unless you know what you're looking for. A few you'll have to share with fellow explorers, a lot you'll likely have all to yourself.

Of course, there are thousands of brilliant places, hidden and otherwise, that don't feature in these pages but this book aims to inspire you with a list of useful and surprising suggestions. It's the spark – the starting place from which to begin an English adventure and discover your own hidden gems along the way.

ABOUT THE AUTHOR

Ellie Walker-Arnott lives in Winchester, Hampshire with her husband Tom, their toddler Evie, baby Violet and cat Ginger. She works as a freelance writer and editor, and is also the author of *Nostalgic London* (Luster). She was previously Time Out's Travel Editor, a job which allowed her to discover hundreds of hidden and lesser-known corners of the country.

After spending years exploring England – from the country's creative hotspots and buzzy beer gardens to its weather-beaten coastline and atmospheric ancient monuments – writing this book has been both an honour and an absolute treat. Populated with Ellie's personal favourites as well as treasures uncovered while hunting around for places to feature, the creation of this book was a joyful reminder that there are always more under-the-radar places to discover in this small but special country.

Ellie would like to thank all the wonderful people, both friends and strangers, who eagerly offered up their recommendations and shared their knowledge of England's hidden gems with her. Thanks to Dettie at Luster for her continued support and to Sam for travelling to every corner of the country to photograph this book. Thanks especially to Mum for looking after Evie so brilliantly and giving Ellie time to write this book, and thanks, as always, to Tom for being an enthusiastic travel companion on English adventures over the years.

HOW TO USE THIS BOOK

This guide lists over 340 places to visit and things to do in England or things to know about the country, that are presented in different categories.

We have included practical information such as the address (including the county) the phone number and the website where these are available. For the purpose of this guide England has been divided into 6 regions, each with its own map; all of these maps can be found at the beginning of the book. Each address is numbered from 1 to 349 and the region corresponding to the map is provided in the description. This will help you to find the address on the right map. A word of caution however: these maps will help you get orientated, but aren't detailed enough to allow you to locate specific places. A good map can be obtained from the local tourist information centre or from most hotels, and you can use your smartphone to locate the addresses.

The author wishes to emphasise that cities and countries are always subject to change. England is no different in this respect. A delicious meal at a restaurant may not taste quite as good on the day that you visit it, a small museum with irregular opening hours might be closed when you knock on the door, or some locations might be difficult to find. But ultimately you may come across something wonderful. This personal and subjective selection is based on the author's experience, at the time of compilation. If you want to add a comment, suggest a correction or recommend a place, please contact the editor at *info@lusterpublishing.com*, or get in touch on Instagram or Facebook *@500hiddensecrets*.

DISCOVER MORE ONLINE

Hidden England is part of the internationally successful travel guide series called *The 500 Hidden Secrets*. The series covers over 40 destinations and includes city guides, regional guides and guides that focus on a specific theme.

Curious about the other destinations? Or looking for inspiration for your next city trip? Visit THE500HIDDENSECRETS.COM. Here you can order every guide from our online shop and find tons of interesting travel content.

Also, don't forget to follow us on Instagram or Facebook for dreamy travel photos and ideas, as well as up-to-date information. Our socials are the easiest way to get in touch with us: we love hearing from you and appreciate all feedback.

the500hiddensecrets

@500hiddensecrets   #500hiddensecrets

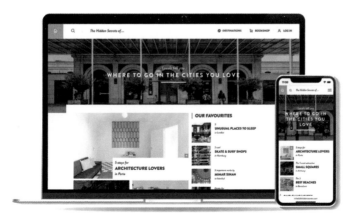

ENGLAND

1 SOUTH WEST

Lundy •

Lynmouth • • Lynton

• Exford

Mouthmill • • Peppercombe
Hartland Quay • • Clovelly

Bude •

Crackington Haven •

Trethevy • • Boscastle
• Trebarwith Strand

Harlyn •
• Bedruthan
• Mount

St Agnes •

New Mill •
St Buryan • • Marazion
• Penzance
• Porthcurno
— Nanjizal Beach
• Lizard

• Pentewan

• Porthcurnick Beach

• Mawgan

DEVON

Okehampton
Spreyton
Drewsteignton

EXETER

• Lydford

• Dartmoor NP
• Two Bridges

Buckfastleigh •

Galmpton •
Kingswear •

South Milton • • Hallsands

Exmouth •

CORNWALL

Lewannick •

• Isles of Scilly

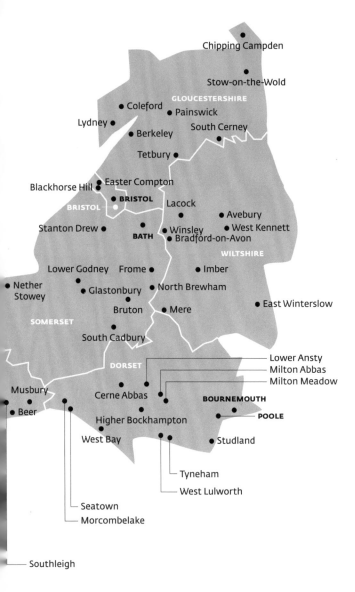

Chipping Campden

Stow-on-the-Wold

GLOUCESTERSHIRE

Coleford
Painswick

Lydney
Berkeley
South Cerney

Tetbury

Blackhorse Hill
Easter Compton

BRISTOL

BRISTOL
Lacock

Avebury

Stanton Drew
Winsley
West Kennett

BATH
Bradford-on-Avon

WILTSHIRE

Lower Godney
Frome
Imber

Nether
Stowey
Glastonbury
North Brewham

Bruton
Mere
East Winterslow

SOMERSET

South Cadbury

DORSET

Lower Ansty
Milton Abbas
Milton Meadow

Musbury
Cerne Abbas
BOURNEMOUTH

Beer
POOLE

Higher Bockhampton

West Bay
Studland

Tyneham

West Lulworth

Seatown

Morcombelake

Southleigh

2 SOUTH EAST

Milton
Keynes

• Little Rollright

Buckingham

**BUCKINGHAM-
SHIRE**

Woodstock •

OXFORD

AYLESBURY

Kelmscott •

OXFORDSHIRE

• Faringdon

• Uffington

Forty Green •

BERKSHIRE

• Donnington **READING**

Hungerford

• Laverstoke

HAMPSHIRE
Farnham

• Fullerton

Chawton •

• Alresford
Winchester • • Cheriton

• Romsey

Buriton •

Petworth

South Graffha
Harting

Halnake

• Lyndhurst

• Brockenhurst

PORTSMOUTH

Bracklesham
Bay

Colwell Bay • **ISLE OF WIGHT**

Arundel —

• Ventnor

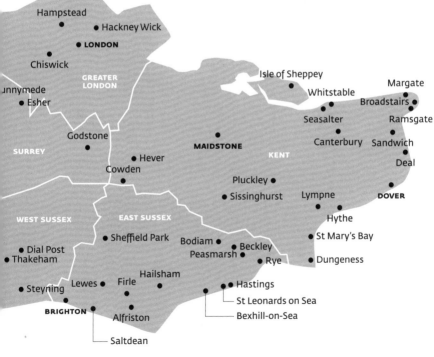

3 EAST OF ENGLAND

4 CENTRAL ENGLAND

Hathersage
Bakewell
Grindleford
Cromford
Edale
High Peak
Castleton
Buxton
Monsal Head
Gradback
Stanton in Peak
Wetton
Alstonefield
Consall
Ashbourne
Creswell
Sutton Scarsdale
NOTTINGHAM-SHIRE
NOTTINGHAM
Cleethorpes
Kirton in Lindsey
Gainsborough
Anderby Creek
Chapel St Leonards
LINCOLNSHIRE
DERBYSHIRE
Moreton Corbet
STAFFORDSHIRE
Ticknall
Loughborough
Grimsthorpe
SHROPSHIRE
Wroxeter
RUTLAND
Church Stretton
LEICESTER
LEICESTERSHIRE
Clun
Chorley
WEST MIDLANDS
Astley
Foxton
BIRMINGHAM
NORTHAMPTON-SHIRE
Tenbury Wells
WARWICKSHIRE
HEREFORDSHIRE
Dorstone
WORCESTER-SHIRE
Lower Maescoed

5 NORTH WEST

CUMBRIA

Cockermouth ●
● Blencowe
Underskiddaw ●
● Dufton
● Keswick
Borrowdale ●
● Orton
Grasmere ●
Tarn Hows ● Ambleside
Eskdale ● ● ● Windermere
Coniston ●
Barngates ———
Hawkshead ———
● Kendal
● Slack Head
Cartmel

Islands of Furness ●
● **LANCASTER**

LANCASHIRE
● Downham
● Barley
● Padiham

Formby ●
GREATER MANCHESTER

MERSEYSIDE
LIVERPOOL ●
Prescot ●
MANCHESTER ●

● Great Budworth

● Chester
● Lower Withington
● Congleton

CHESHIRE

6 NORTH EAST

LAVENHAM

SCALLOP BY MAGGI HAMBLING

ART and CULTURE Ⓐ

Art in **SURPRISING PLACES**

1 **LIGHT PYRAMID**
AT: CAMPBELL PARK
**Midsummer
Boulevard
Milton Keynes,
Buckinghamshire
MK9 3FT
South East**

The relatively new town of Milton Keynes, which was founded in the 1960s, might be better known for its shopping centre and indoor ski resort, but the entire town was actually designed around the movement of the sun. It's built around a neat grid pattern that aligns with the sunrise on the summer solstice – the longest day of the year – and the *Light Pyramid*, an eye-catching white sculpture by Liliane Lijn (2012) made out of steel, in Campbell Park also marks this point.

2 **SCALLOP**
**Aldeburgh Beach
Suffolk
IP16 4NR
East of England**

A giant steel scallop shell sits on the pebble beach at Aldeburgh in Suffolk, one half standing upright while the other leans onto the stones. If you're filled with the desire to climb or use the shell as a seat for eating chips or staring out into the waves, go right ahead. The sculptor Maggi Hambling wanted passersby to physically interact with the shell. The whimsical design is a tribute to the composer Benjamin Britten, who lived in Aldeburgh, and is inscribed with the words "I hear those voices that will not be drowned", which is a quote from one of Britten's operas.

3 WRIT IN WATER

AT: RUNNYMEDE
NATURE RESERVE
Windsor Road
Runnymede,
Surrey
SL4 2JL
South East
+44 (0)17 8443 2891
nationaltrust.org.uk

The Magna Carta is one of the most famous, historic documents in the world. The charter of rights and liberties was signed by King John in 1215 in Runnymede, Surrey – and the place is now considered by many to be the birthplace of modern democracy. To mark that ancient legacy, the artwork *Writ in Water* by Mark Wallinger (2018) was installed in a quiet, rural spot. Inside the circular structure beside the River Thames, the sky is visible through a round opening above a pool of still water. Reversed and inverted words from the Magna Carta are inscribed on the edge of the pool, only legible when read reflected in the water.

4 COLDSTONES CUT

Greenhow Hill,
North Yorkshire
HG3 5JL
North East
thecoldstonescut.org

Talk about an unusual location for a public work of art. *Coldstones Cut* by Andrew Sabin (2010) is high on a hill in the Nidderdale AONB (Area of Outstanding Natural Beauty), above a huge working limestone quarry. The mammoth sculpture, which visitors can walk around through enclosed paths and open platforms, is designed to be both a place to view the quarry and admire the beautiful rural landscape which surrounds it.

Weird and wonderful
COLLECTIONS

---

5 **MUSEUM OF WITCHCRAFT AND MAGIC**
AT: THE HARBOUR
**Boscastle,
Cornwall
PL35 0HD
South West**
*museumofwitchcraft
andmagic.co.uk*

An unassuming white building in coastal Boscastle's pretty harbour, near fish and chip shops and gift stores, is home to an incredible collection of surprising artefacts. Exploring British magical practices, from ancient times to the modern day, the miniature museum is stuffed full of beguiling items. We're talking cauldrons, crystal balls and wands, tarot cards and talismans, charms for protection and poppets for curses. A glimpse in a witch mirror will change your relationship with reflective surfaces forever (if you gaze into it, you might suddenly see someone standing behind you, though you must never turn around!). You're guaranteed to lose all track of time during a wander through the museum – and likely to leave with a good luck charm from the shop in your pocket. You know, just in case.

6 **DERWENT PENCIL MUSEUM**
**Southey Works
Keswick,
Cumbria
CA12 5NG
North West
+44 (0)17 6877 3626**
derwentart.com

If you're a firm believer that you can't beat a fresh HB pencil, you will be in your element in this little museum in the Lake District. This is the home of the world's first pencil. Derwent have been making pencils in Keswick since 1832 using graphite mined from the local area. Find miniature pencil sculptures, see one of the biggest colour pencils in the world and don't miss the shop, to stock up on tins of soft sketching pencils for your own collection.

5 MUSEUM OF WITCHCRAFT AND MAGIC

6 DERWENT PENCIL MUSEUM

7 DOG COLLAR MUSEUM

AT: LEEDS CASTLE
Maidstone,
Kent
ME17 1RG
South East
+44 (0)16 2276 5400
leeds-castle.com

Dog people will appreciate this unique collection of collars worn by pooches over the centuries. There are 130 rare dog collars on display here, ranging from iron collars adorned with sharp spikes to fancy, fine silver ones. Visitors can spy collars from the 15th century onwards. The diminutive museum currently houses the largest display of its kind on the planet – the collection is continuing to grow, too, with members of the public donating unusual collars to the castle.

8 THE OSSUARY

AT: ST LEONARD'S
CHURCH
Oak Walk
Hythe,
Kent
CT21 5DN
South East
slhk.org

This one is a little on the macabre side. A church in Kent is home to the largest and best-preserved collection of ancient human skulls and bones in the country. The ossuary is estimated to contain the remains of around 2000 people, though who they are and how they found themselves here remains unclear. The skeletons – shelves of skulls and one large stack of bones – are thought to date from around the 13th century. Studies are ongoing to determine the stories of the people who call this crypt their final resting place.

SCULPTURE GARDENS
and trails

9 **KIELDER ART AND ARCHITECTURE**
AT: KIELDER WATER
& FOREST PARK
Kielder,
Northumberland
NE48 1BT
North East
+44 (0)84 5155 0236
visitkielder.com

You'll find a number of alfresco artworks in the landscape around Northumberland's Kielder Water and Forest Park. The collection has grown over the last three decades to create free rural walking routes dotted with sculptures and installations. There are a number of architectural shelters and spaces to be found too, including *Kielder Belvedere* by Softroom Architects (1999), a mirrored, lake-side cabin that disappears into its surroundings and *Silvas Capitalis* by SIMPARCH (2009), a huge wooden head on the forest floor – visitors can step inside its gaping mouth and climb a set of internal stairs to view the woodland through its eyes. Literally.

10 **NEW ART CENTRE**
Roche Court
East Winterslow,
Wiltshire
SP5 1BG
South West
+44 (0)19 8086 2244
sculpture.uk.com

Set over 60 acres of Wiltshire parkland, the New Art Centre provides a bucolic setting for 20th and 21st-century works of art. The grounds of Roche Court, and a stretch of bluebell woodland, are dotted with sculptures, some that contrast and some that blend in with their rural setting. You'll find works from world-renowned artists here and they're all for sale, if your bank balance is healthy enough.

11 TREMENHEERE SCULPTURE GARDENS

**Penzance,
Cornwall
TR20 8YL
South West
+44 (0)17 3644 8089
tremenheere.co.uk**

Tucked away in a peaceful spot near Penzance, this subtropical sculpture garden reveals surprise after surprise. Visitors wander uphill into the gardens, past trickling streams and the vivid greens of freshly uncurled fern fronds, to discover sculptures woven into the landscape. Some blend in, made of organic, earthy materials, while others boldly stand out from their surroundings. The gardens are slightly inland, but you can glimpse wonderful sea views across to St Michael's Mount from Tremenheere's highest point. Don't miss *Tewlwolow Kernow* by James Turrell (2013), a domed, circular chamber open to the elements from which to view the sky.

12 YORKSHIRE SCULPTURE PARK

**West Bretton,
West Yorkshire
WF4 4LG
North East
+44 (0)19 2483 2631
ysp.org.uk**

If you're big into sculpture you might have heard of Yorkshire Sculpture Park. It's been showcasing the best in outdoor art for 45 years and is the largest of its kind in Europe. But there are surprises to be found here even for the most seasoned culture fans. The park is set within a 500-acre estate, made up of formal gardens as well as wilder woodland. World-class artworks sit within the rural landscape waiting to be discovered. Hunt out pieces by Ai Weiwei, Antony Gormley, Henry Moore, Barbara Hepworth and more – there are hidden wonders here wherever you look.

13 **FOREST OF DEAN SCULPTURE TRAIL**
AT: BEECHENHURST
Speech House Road
Coleford,
Gloucestershire
GL16 7EL
South West
+44 (0)30 0067 4800
forestofdean-
sculpture.org.uk

The ancient Forest of Dean contains four miles of carefully curated artworks, hidden among the trees. Each installation is designed to be explored by passersby, and are intended to reflect or comment on their setting. All the artworks have been developed on location and are inspired by the forest they live within. Look out for *Cone and Vessel* by Peter Randall-Page (1988), a supersized pinecone and acorn cup carved from local stone, and *Cathedral* by Kevin Atherton (1986), a large stained-glass window suspended in the branches above walkers' heads.

Surprising ART GALLERIES

14 SALTS MILL
Victoria Road
Saltaire,
West Yorkshire
BD18 3LA
North East
+44 (0)12 7453 1163
saltsmill.org.uk

Built in 1853 as a huge textile mill, Salts Mill was once the largest industrial building in the world. Since its closure in the 1980s, the historic building has taken on a new identity as a mega art gallery, with shops and restaurants on site. As well as having a huge collection of works by local artist David Hockney, Salts Mill hosts regularly changing exhibitions from other artists, all of which are free to explore.

15 KETTLES YARD
Castle St
Cambridge,
Cambridgeshire
CB3 0AQ
East of England
+44 (0)12 2374 8100
kettlesyard.co.uk

Owned by the University of Cambridge, Kettle's Yard is a beautiful house filled with wonderful objects and modern art, plus an extension, which houses a contemporary art gallery. Amazingly, the house – which was the home of Jim Ede, a former Tate Gallery curator, and his wife Helen – was donated in its entirety to the university in the 1960s. It's been left just as the Edes lived in it, and visitors are invited to wander freely through its carefully curated rooms.

16 HAUSER & WIRTH

AT: DURSLADE FARM
Dropping Lane
Bruton,
Somerset
BA10 0NL
South West
+44 (0)17 4981 4060
hauserwirth.com

Hauser & Wirth have outposts in New York, LA, London, Hong Kong and… the tiny town of Bruton in Somerset. Bruton is way cooler than your average rural outpost, but it still feels surreal to stumble upon such a good art gallery here, essentially surrounded by farmland. Both the gallery and its dreamy garden – the highlight of which is the expansive landscape-designed meadow Oudolf Field and its resident, otherworldly Radić Pavilion – are totally free to enter. Visit for thought-provoking exhibitions, and to lose yourself among grasses and blooms in the meadow.

17 HASTINGS CONTEMPORARY

Rock-a-Nore Road
Hastings,
East Sussex
TN34 3DW
South East
+44 (0)14 2472 8377
hastings
contemporary.org

Right on the stones besides Hastings' tall, wooden fishing net huts, Hastings Contemporary is a small gallery full of bright coastal light. For a little gallery it draws in big talent, hosting exhibitions and installations that sometimes nod to its beachfront location. The illustrator Sir Quentin Blake is Artist Patron of the gallery, so expect to find examples of his work on the walls, and original paintings and drawings for sale in the gallery shop.

Atmospheric
ARTISTS' HOUSES

18 **GREENWAY HOUSE AND GARDEN**
Greenway Road
Galmpton,
Devon
TQ5 0ES
South West
+44 (0)18 0384 2382
nationaltrust.org.uk

Tucked away in a secluded spot besides the River Dart sits Agatha Christie's former holiday home. It was the site of happy occasions far removed from the dark contents of her murder mystery novels (though the Boathouse does appear in her novel *Dead Man's Folly*). Inside the grand white house you'll find bright rooms filled with treasures: books, archaeological finds, porcelain figures, ceramics and curiosities. Outside, walled gardens and rambling woodland lead down to the water's edge.

19 **CHARLESTON**
Firle,
East Sussex
BN8 6LL
South East
+44 (0)13 2381 1626
charleston.org.uk

Charleston – the former home of painters Vanessa Bell and Duncan Grant, and a meeting place for the progressive writers, artists and thinkers who made up the Bloomsbury Group – is a work of art in itself. After moving from London to the rural house in 1916 around the outbreak of WWI, Bell and Grant set about painting every internal wall and surface. The result is an arty, atmospheric home filled with intriguing objects and creative corners. You can wander freely around the perfectly preserved house and garden. You'll also find exhibitions in Charleston's gallery space and a buzzy events calendar of small festivals, short courses, performances, talks and hands-on creative workshops, if a visit here leaves you feeling inspired.

20 COLERIDGE COTTAGE

35 Lime St
Nether Stowey,
Somerset
TA5 1NQ
South West
+44 (0)12 7873 2662
nationaltrust.org.uk

It's as though the poet Samuel Taylor Coleridge has just stepped out of the house at his former home in the little village of Nether Stowey. Each of the rooms in the little lemon-coloured cottage have been set up as they might have been when Coleridge and his family lived here in the 1790s. If you feel inspired to put pen to paper here, you won't be surprised to discover that it was within these four walls that the famous Romantic poet wrote some of his most loved works including *The Rime of the Ancient Mariner.*

21 HARDY'S COTTAGE

Higher
Bockhampton,
Dorset
DT2 8QJ
South West
+44 (0)13 0526 2366
nationaltrust.org.uk

It's easy to imagine you've stepped from the page into Thomas Hardy's bucolic Wessex here. This tiny cob and thatch cottage is where the author was born in 1840 and it remains largely as it was when his family lived here. You can explore the evocative cottage garden, as well as the cottage's rooms with their open hearths and creaky floorboards. For more Hardy, head to Max Gate, the grander home Hardy built himself and later died in – it's just three miles away on the outskirts of Dorchester.

22 PROSPECT COTTAGE

Dungeness Road
Dungeness,
Kent
TN29 9NE
South East
creative
folkestone.org.uk

Artist, filmmaker and activist Derek Jarman moved to this desert-like corner of Kent in the 1980s, and this black and yellow timber cottage remained his home and workspace until his death in 1994. Preserved by his close friend Keith Collins for a number of years, it's now in the care of Creative Folkstone, who maintain the inspiring space and the beautiful, shingle garden Jarman created.

23 JANE AUSTEN'S HOUSE

**Chawton,
Hampshire
GU34 1SD
South East
+44 (0)14 2083 262
*janeaustens.house***

Jane Austen might be more famously associated with the city of Bath, with its fancy, regency architecture and museum dedicated to the author. Few know that she actually spent much of her life in Hampshire. She was born in Steventon and spent the last eight years of her life in the small village of Chawton. Here, surrounded by Hampshire countryside, she wrote *Emma* and *Persuasion*, among others, while *Pride and Prejudice* and *Sense and Sensibility* were published. Visitors will find Austen's letters, first editions and even her writing table. Nearby Winchester is also worth a visit for Austen fans – she died there, in a townhouse on College Street, in 1817 and is buried in the city's cathedral.

22 PROSPECT COTTAGE

24 DOVE COTTAGE

Grasmere,
Cumbria
LA22 9SH
North West
+44 (0)15 3943 5544
wordsworth.org.uk

A neat white cottage in the rural wilds of the Lake District, this was once the home of poet William Wordsworth and his family. He described his house here on the outskirts of Grasmere as 'the loveliest spot man hath ever found', and it's easy to see why. Dove Cottage has now been restored and is set in scenes inspired by Wordsworth's writing and his sister Dorothy's journals. Visitors can explore each room of the cottage and 'wander lonely as a cloud' through its surrounding garden, orchard and woodland. Nearby Rydal Mount, the home where Wordsworth lived from 1813 until his death, is also worth a visit.

25 KELMSCOTT MANOR

Kelmscott,
Oxfordshire
GL7 3HJ
South East
+44 (0)13 6725 2486
sal.org.uk

There is no doubt some of William Morris's iconic designs were inspired by the lush countryside and gardens that surround Kelmscott Manor. The artist, a leader of the Arts and Crafts movement, rented the stunning Cotswolds manor from 1871 until his death in 1896. Morris described the place, which he secured as a rural retreat from London for his family, as heaven on earth. All three floors of the grand 17th-century home are open for the public to explore, along with dreamy gardens which have been restored to their former glory, planted with blooms from Morris's writing and designs.

Amazing **THEATRES**

26 **THE GRANGE AT NORTHINGTON**

Alresford,
Hampshire
SO24 9TZ
South East
+44 (0)19 6279 1020
thegrange
festival.co.uk

A rough country track leads to The Grange, a 17th-century building that, thanks to a 19th-century renovation, resembles a grand Greek temple. The Grecian-inspired construction, which is dominated by eight enormous columns, is a little out of place in the pretty Hampshire valley it presides over. But it's popular with locals, who campaigned successfully to save it from demolition in the 1970s. These days it's taken over each summer by The Grange Festival and becomes the spectacular setting for a season of opera performances. Ticket-holders can sip The Grange sparkling wine on the portico, and enjoy fine dining or a BYO picnic on the grass in the performance interval. The Grange's grounds are also open daily and free to enter all year round, thanks to English Heritage.

27 **SHAKESPEARE NORTH PLAYHOUSE**

Prospero Place
Prescot,
Merseyside
L34 3AB
North West
+44 (0)15 1433 7156
shakespearenorth
playhouse.co.uk

Opened in 2022, this brand-new performance space is based on the Shakespearean theatre Cockpit-in-Court, which was built in 1533 for Henry VIII in part of Whitehall Palace in London. The action is in a wooden round, but unlike the world-famous Globe Theatre on the capital's South Bank, it is covered from the elements. Expect traditional as well as innovative takes on the bard's classic plays, as well as modern productions and performances.

28 THE MINACK THEATRE

**Porthcurno,
Cornwall
TR19 6JU
South West
+44 (0)17 3681 0181**
minack.com

It's not hyperbole to say this theatre is one of the most magical in the world. Perched high on a Cornish clifftop, with mind-boggling views of the Atlantic Ocean, the open-air theatre is literally cut into the rugged landscape. It was built, almost entirely by hand, by landowner Rowena Cade and her two gardeners, first for a 1932 performance of *The Tempest* before being improved and expanded. Most of the theatre's terraces are built out of concrete, inscribed with words and Cornish symbols. You can explore the otherworldly theatre and its gardens year round, but you can catch all kinds of plays and performances here in the warmer months, from touring stand-up and productions straight from the West End to shows from local choirs. All take place with the watery horizon, and, if you're lucky, a sunset, as their backdrop. Performances are only cancelled in extreme weather – and umbrellas are not permitted – so arrive prepared to face the elements!

29 THEATRE BY THE LAKE

AT: LAKESIDE
**Keswick,
Cumbria
CA12 5DJ
North West
+44 (0)17 6877 4411**
theatrebythelake.com

On the peaceful shores of Derwentwater, next to rows of bobbing rental boats, is Theatre by the Lake. Visitors will be treated to lush views of the lake and its surrounding fells, as well as a buzzy programme of performances. Their calendar is made up of touring shows, in-house productions and work from local theatre clubs.

30 **THE GEORGIAN THEATRE ROYAL**
Victoria Road Richmond, North Yorkshire DL10 4DW North East +44 (0)17 4882 5252 *georgiantheatre royal.co.uk*

Richmond is home to the most complete Georgian playhouse in England. Built in 1788, it's still a working theatre today, hosting comedy, musical performances and a much-loved panto each winter. You can book tours during the day when the stage is empty to get up close with this historic space, which includes a woodland set that is England's oldest surviving example of stage scenery, too.

31 **TOM THUMB THEATRE**
2-A Eastern Esplanade Margate, Kent CT9 2LB South East +44 (0)18 4322 1791 *tomthumb theatre.co.uk*

Seating just 50, Margate's Tom Thumb Theatre is one of the smallest in the world. The building was originally a Victorian coach house, but it's now a charming community arts hub and welcoming bar open for pre and post-theatre drinks. This diminutive spot boasts a diverse line-up. Visit for stellar stand-up, spoken word and musical performances.

Showstopping **CINEMAS**

---

32 **TIVOLI BATH**

6-8 Dorchester St
Bath,
Somerset
BA1 1SS
South West
tivolicinemas.com

You could happily move right into this plush, design-led cinema. It's as captivating to look at as the movie you're there to see. Seats are squishy, roomy sofas, where you can order meals for in-screen dining. The bar is open all day, serving coffee and pastries in the morning through to mezze and cocktails in the evening. Basically, there's no need to go anywhere else.

33 **PRINCE CHARLES CINEMA**

7 Leicester Place
London
WC2H 7BY
South East
+44 (0)20 7494 3654
princecharles
cinema.com

Leicester Square in central London is known for its big, multi-plex, movie-premiere-hosting cinemas, but if you step a little off the main square you'll find a smaller cinema that is more worth your time. The Prince Charles Cinema is the last independent cinema left in the West End. You don't come to this two-screener to watch the latest Marvel movie, you come to see all-time classic films and B-movies you've never seen before, to sit through an all-night horror movie marathon or watch five festive films screened back-to-back at a Christmas Pyjama Party. They also put on interactive screenings where you can sing along with musical numbers without annoying the person next to you. Perfection.

A

34 THE STATION CINEMA

AT: RICHMOND STATION
**Station Yard
Richmond,
North Yorkshire
DL10 4LD
North East
+44 (0)17 4882 3062**
stationcinema.com

It might still look a lot like the place to begin a journey on the rails, but the last train passed through Richmond's Victorian train station in 1968. It's now an atmospheric cinema, showing modern releases as well as cult favourites and film festivals. To really embrace the cinema's history, book onto their annual, festive screening of *The Polar Express* – hot chocolate and sweet snacks are included in the ticket price.

35 LYNTON CINEMA

**Lee Road
Lynton,
Devon
EX35 6HN
South West
+44 (0)15 9875 3397**
lyntoncinema.co.uk

A trip to this old converted Methodist chapel in the tiny coastal town of Lynton feels a bit like stepping back in time a decade or... nine. Visitors to the Grade II-listed picture palace are guaranteed to be treated to the latest releases, though. Lynton only has a population of around 2000 people and is thought to be the smallest town in the country to boast a full-time cinema.

36 THE ULTIMATE PICTURE PALACE

**Jeune St, Cowley Rd
Oxford,
Oxfordshire
OX4 1BN
South East
+44 (0)18 6524 5288**
uppcinema.com

This little gem of a cinema, which first opened in 1911 is owned by the local community, who banded together to save it when the previous owner passed away. It just has one screening room, plus a bar for stocking up on locally made movie snacks. Tickets are purchased retro style, from the original box office window which is open to the street.

37 HAILSHAM PAVILION

George St
Hailsham,
East Sussex
BN27 1AE
South East
+44 (0)13 2384 1414
hailsham
pavilion.co.uk

It's a good job the lights are down low during film screenings at Hailsham's glorious cinema or you might find yourself gazing at the 1920s-style interiors instead. Built in 1921, this historic picture palace has recently been restored to reflect how it looked during its heyday. It's now a charming and intimate place to see new films, as well as live events and festivals.

38 KINO RYE

Lion St
Rye,
East Sussex
TN31 7LB
South East
+44 (0)17 9722 6293
kinodigital.co.uk

You wouldn't expect to find a cinema on the medieval streets of Rye, beside half-timbered houses and ancient pubs. Kino Rye is a petite cinema tucked away from Rye's busy cobbles in a former Victorian library, with two intimate screening rooms. There's also a pretty outside terrace for debriefing after the credits roll.

THE LONG BENCH

DISCOVER 🔍

UNDERGROUND *marvels*

39 SHELL GROTTO

Grotto Hill
Margate,
Kent
CT9 2BU
South East
+44 (0)18 4322 0008
shellgrotto.co.uk

Hidden beneath the streets of Margate in Kent, the Shell Grotto is a bewitching, dreamlike space. Pass through an unassuming entrance in a quiet residential part of the seaside town before heading down below street level where you're met with a warren of underground passages, all lined with softly gleaming seashells. The shells – 4,6 million of them, mainly British and found locally – are set into the chalk in beautifully patterned mosaics. Why? Who knows. The grotto was discovered by chance in 1835 and its origins remain unknown to this day, though theories range from an ancient pagan temple to an extravagant, Regency folly. See what you think when you step inside.

40 BEER QUARRY CAVES

Quarry Lane
Beer,
Devon
EX12 3AS
South West
+44 (0)12 9768 0282
*beerquarry
caves.co.uk*

You'll want to wrap up warm for a trip down Beer's Quarry Caves, even if it's beach weather above ground. The cool, man-made labyrinth of underground tunnels is the result of over 2000 years of quarrying Beer Stone. The Romans were the first to start using the creamy limestone, but it's since featured in famous buildings like Westminster Abbey and The Tower of London. You can now take a tour of the vast underground caverns (which are also popular with bat populations) near the pretty village of Beer.

41 ROYSTON CAVE

Melbourn St
Royston,
Hertfordshire
SG8 7BZ
East of England
+44 (0)17 6324 2587
roystoncave.co.uk

Concealed beneath the pavements in the centre of Royston, this subterranean space really is a surprise. Uncovered by workers in 1742, Royston Cave is a beehive-shaped chamber decorated with extensive wall carvings that are thought to be medieval, dating back to the 1300s. The cave's exact age and purpose, though, remain unknown as no records exist. A secret place of worship used by the Knights Templar, or an early Freemason's Lodge? A sacred space where two Ley lines meet? Your guess is as good as any.

42 THE KELVEDON HATCH SECRET NUCLEAR BUNKER

Kelvedon Hall Lane
Kelvedon Hatch,
Essex
CM14 5TL
East of England
+44 (0)12 7736 4883
*secretnuclear
bunker.com*

The huge underground bunker at Kelvedon Hatch has had a varied history. Built in the 1950s as an RAF ROTOR air defence station, it was maintained by the government during the Cold War as emergency regional government headquarters. It could have housed around 600 military and civilian personnel – and maybe even the Prime Minister – in the event of nuclear war. The site was decommissioned in the 1990s and you can now take self-guided tours through the atmospheric space.

43 FAN BAY DEEP SHELTER

AT: LANGDON CLIFFS
Upper Road
Dover,
Kent
CT16 1HJ
South East
+44 (0)13 0420 7326
nationaltrust.org.uk

Hard hats and head torches are required (and provided) when you venture down the 125 steep steps into Fan Bay Deep Shelter. You'll need sturdy footwear too to get you around the underground tunnel complex. In fact, you'll need good shoes just to get you to the entrance, which is a 45-minute walk from the nearest car park at Dover's famous white cliffs. This abandoned shelter, deep inside Kent's famous white chalk cliffs, was constructed in 1940 and provided bomb-proof accommodation for the gun battery above. Now it is all that remains of the former WWII defence.

44 MEGATRON AND SHEAF CULVERTS

Sheffield,
South Yorkshire
S1 4SQ
North East
sheafportertrust.org

Tours exploring hidden sections of the River Sheaf, a modest river which has flowed through the heart of Sheffield for centuries, sell out super quickly. The river has largely become hidden underground, channelled into culverts to be used in industry or to make way for construction. The Sheaf and Porter Rivers Trust are promoting the re-naturalisation of Sheffield's rivers, and part of that involves running these urban caving tours, where visitors can walk the underground route of the river, finishing up in the Megatron, an enormous, cave-like Victorian storm drain with a sweeping curved roof.

Amazing **MAZES**

45 **WATER MAZE**

AT: HEVER CASTLE
AND GARDENS
Hever,
Kent
TN8 7NG
South East
+44 (0)17 3286 5224
hevercastle.co.uk

You might want to bring a change of clothes, or at least a towel, to take on the Water Maze. Few make it to the stone grotto at the centre without getting wet. The unusual puzzle is made up of stepping stones sitting over water. One wrong step and your stepping stone could tilt, soaking you thanks to the water jets hidden below. Once you've dried off, stick around to explore Hever Castle – it was once the childhood home of Henry VIII's second wife Anne Boleyn.

46 MARLBOROUGH MAZE

AT: BLENHEIM PALACE
Woodstock,
Oxfordshire
OX20 1UL
South East
+44 (0)19 9381 0530
blenheimpalace.com

Tucked away within walled gardens in Blenheim Palace's palatial grounds, the Marlborough Maze is a classic hedge maze. It's made up of hundreds of yew trees that have been sculpted into two miles (3,2 kilometres) of swirling, curving pathways that lead to the centre. There are two bridges if you need a little perspective to find your way.

47 THE MAZE

AT: CHATSWORTH
Bakewell,
Derbyshire
DE45 1PP
Central England
+44 (0)12 4656 5300
chatsworth.org

The Maze is actually one of the newest additions to Chatsworth, a much-loved, 17th-century stately home and estate in Derbyshire. Constructed on the site of a Great Conservatory in the 1960s, the labyrinth was made possible by the planting of more than 1209 English yews. Climb the Hundred Steps beside the hedges for a view from which to plot your route.

48 MINOTAUR MAZE

AT: KIELDER CASTLE
Kielder,
Northumberland
NE48 1ER
North East
+44 (0)14 3425 0209
forestryengland.uk

Built from basalt stone with a recycled glass box at its heart, the Minotaur Maze in the grounds of Northumberland's Kielder Castle isn't your average maze. The angular construction also features internal windows and a set of stairs for spying on your fellow players. Or for working out how to retrace your steps, once you've reached the maze's glittering centre.

MAGICAL *and*
MYSTICAL *spots*

49 **MERMAID'S POOL**
High Peak,
Derbyshire
SK22 2LJ
Central England

A glassy pool on the slopes below Kinder Scout, the highest point in the Peak District, Mermaid's Pool is a great spot to take a dip and admire the views. It's also, according to legend, a body of water with healing properties, and even somewhere you can be gifted eternal life. You just have to go for a swim at midnight on Easter Sunday, as that's when the pool's resident mermaid is said to appear. If you catch her in the right mood, immortality is yours. Winner!

50 **CHALICE WELL**
85-89 Chilkwell St
Glastonbury,
Somerset
BA6 8DD
South West
+44 (0)14 5883 1154
chalicewell.org.uk

Glastonbury is one of the most well-known spiritual spots in England. Its iconic Tor, topped by a 15th-century tower, is steeped in mystery, and is popular with pagans and the spiritually curious all year round. Tucked away at the bottom of the hill, in a pretty walled garden, sits the lesser-known Chalice Well. Here you'll find an ancient natural spring, known as the Red Spring because the water runs a reddish shade, that is thought to have healing qualities if you're brave enough to take a sip. Either way, the gardens are a peaceful place to stop and pause.

51 ST NECTAN'S GLEN

Trethevy,
Cornwall
PL34 0BE
South West
+44 (0)18 4077 9538
st-nectansglen.co.uk

Said to be home to fairies and spirits as well as, at one point, St Nectan himself, this enchanting woodland near Cornwall's famous clifftop castle Tintagel is one of England's most sacred sites. Wander along the River Trevillet to St Nectan's Kieve, a stunning waterfall that has cut a neat circle in the rock, and you'll soon feel why. The area at the bottom of the waterfall is adorned with ribbons, crystals and devotions left by those who have been taken by the area's otherworldly atmosphere. Come prepared with wellies or waterproof shoes (or be prepared to take your shoes off) as you'll need to wander through the stream to see the waterfall.

51 ST NECLAN'S GLEN

52 LUD'S CHURCH

AT: BACK FOREST,
DARK PEAK
Near Gradback,
Staffordshire
SK17 0SU
Central England

It comes as no surprise to learn that this deep, moss-covered cavern is the subject of myth and mystery. Walking down its atmospheric stone steps is like descending into an alternative universe. It's known that the secret space has been used as a place of worship over the centuries, while some say it was created by the devil with a slash of his fingernail.

53 CADBURY CASTLE

South Cadbury,
Somerset
BA22 7HA
South West

Rumour has it that Cadbury Castle was the true location of King Arthur's legendary castle Camelot during the 6th century. Whether or not there's any truth to the Arthurian whispers, Cadbury Castle was definitely an important fortification during that time. Believed to have been constructed in the Bronze Age, this impressive hillfort has seen action from the Roman invasion as well as being a defence against the Vikings. It's now a high point looking out over the Somerset Levels, with the grassy ridges, ditches and earthen ramparts to explore.

54 ARTHUR'S STONE

Arthur's Stone Lane
Dorstone,
Herefordshire
HR3 6AX
Central England
+44 (0)37 0333 1181
english-heritage.org.uk

Another atmospheric place with an Arthurian connection, this neolithic burial chamber perched high on a hill overlooking Herefordshire's Golden Valley has been linked to King Arthur since the 13th century. It's said that the legendary figure fought and slew a giant here. The giant is meant to have left the imprint of his elbow on one of the stones as he fell.

55 **FAIRY STEPS**

Slack Head,
Cumbria
LA7 7BD
North West

According to folklore, fairies themselves have been spotted skipping up and down these tiny steps. Found in a cutting between enormous limestone rocks, the Fairy Steps are a set of natural stone steps. Squeeze up or down the miniature flight of stairs without touching the rocks on either side (a fairly impossible task unless you are fairy-sized) and the fairies are said to grant you a wish. Incredibly, the steps are on a historic corpse trail, a route along which coffins would be carried to a local churchyard. To reach the steps, there's a well-signposted walking route from the nearby village of Beetham.

56 **CHANCTONBURY RING**

AT: SOUTH DOWNS
NATIONAL PARK
Steyning,
West Sussex
BN44 3DR
South East

A prehistoric hill fort crowned with a ring of beech trees that sits high on the South Downs Way, Chanctonbury Ring has been an area of significance since the neolithic age. There are even the remains of two Roman temples here a little below the surface. It's also the focus of intriguing local folklore, which claims the hill was made by the devil, and if you were to run around the circle of trees anti-clockwise seven times the devil would appear and gift you a bowl of soup. That hot meal comes at a high price, though, as it is offered in exchange for your soul.

SEASIDE *secrets*

57 **THE LONG BENCH**

Eastern
Promenade
Littlehampton,
West Sussex
BN17 5LG
South East
longbench.org

The longest bench in England and probably one of the longest in the world, this colourful construction in Littlehampton wiggles and weaves along the seafront. A continuous sweep of wood and stainless steel, the Long Bench curves around obstacles and dips up and down with the beachfront terrain. It is 1000 feet (305 metres) long and can seat 300 people. Touchingly, the bench's wooden slats are also engraved with special messages, commemorating achievements, anniversaries or much-missed loved ones.

57 **THE LONG BENCH**

58 THE CLOUD BAR

Sea Road
Anderby Creek,
Lincolnshire
Central England

If you've always got your head in the clouds, there's finally somewhere for you to while away an afternoon in peace. The Anderby Creek Cloud Bar is the first permanent structure designed for cloud-watching in England. There are seats for reclining on and getting stellar views of the clouds scudding by overhead, cloud mirrors for bringing blue skies down to earth and info boards detailing different cloud classifications and how to identify them.

59 THE UNDER THE PIER SHOW

AT: SOUTHWOLD PIER
Southwold,
Suffolk
IP18 6BN
East of England
+44 (0)15 0272 2105
underthepier.com

Arcade games on an English pier? So far, so standard. Yet there's nothing run of the mill about this surreal set of interactive amusements. Southwold's pier is home to Tim Hunkin's wonderfully eccentric Under the Pier Show. Inside you'll find a series of satirical handmade machines, which include Whack a Banker (instead of the classic Whack a Mole), a zimmer frame simulator and a school run-inspired driving game. Outside, on the pier deck itself, you can also spot The Water Clock, which was made by Hunkin too. The time-keeping sculpture, which was designed to comment on water recycling, sees copper characters put on a pee show every half an hour.

60 DENGE SOUND MIRRORS

AT: LADE PITS RSPB
DUNGENESS NATURE
RESERVE
Seaview Road
Dungeness,
Kent
TN28 8RJ
South East
rspb.org.uk

Dungeness is a bleak but fascinating stretch of the Kent coastline, made up of shingle, grassland and wildflower meadow. It's home to small shacks, lighthouses, architectural creations, a nuclear power station and the Denge Sound Mirrors. The sound mirrors, which are also called listening ears, are three concrete structures ranging in size from 20 to 200 feet (6 to 60 metres), and they are relics of a pre-WWII acoustic defence system. Built between 1928 and 1935, the mirrors were designed to pick up the sound of enemy aircraft approaching over the English Channel. They have long since been replaced by radar systems, and are now scheduled monuments of national importance. They're found in Lade Pits Nature Reserve, which is open daily. You can't always get up close to the sound mirrors – they are on an inaccessible man-made island – but a number of open days are held each year where you can get within whispering distance.

Really DARK SKIES

61 **SURPRISE VIEW**
PARK AT: SURPRISE
VIEW CAR PARK
A6187 Grindleford,
Derbyshire
S32 1DA
Central England

One of the Peak District's three official dark sky sites, Surprise View is a mega viewpoint from which to admire the countryside or set off on a walking trail in daylight hours. Stick around to watch the sunset over the hills. Stay until it's properly dark and, on a clear night, you'll be treated to a twinkly celestial vista overhead too.

62 **BUTSER HILL**
Buriton,
Hampshire
GU31 5SP
South East

The highest point in Hampshire, Butser Hill is an ace place to stargaze thanks to its rural nature reserve location and lack of light pollution. High up on the hill, there is nothing to obstruct your view of the night's sky. It's also slap bang in the middle of the South Downs National Park, which became an International Dark Sky Reserve in 2016, meaning it's a brilliant place to gaze up.

63 **BEDRUTHAN STEPS**
Bedruthan,
Cornwall
PL27 7UW
South West

Clear skies and eager eyes are all you need at Bedruthan Steps, a stretch of remote Cornish coastline that is a brilliant place to spot shooting stars, constellations and even the Milky Way on especially clear nights. The views are pretty stellar during daylight too – this rugged beach between Padstow and Newquay is known for its dramatic rock stacks.

64 NORTHUMBERLAND DARK SKY PARK

Northumberland
North East
*northumberland
nationalpark.org.uk*

There are 572 square miles (920 square kilometres) of countryside primed for gold tier stargazing in Northumberland. You can take your pick of locations as Northumberland's internationally recognised Dark Sky Park spans most of the county including Northumberland National Park and Kielder Water and Forest Park. It's easily the best place in England to stargaze. Just wait until dark and, as long as cloud cover doesn't obstruct your view, you'll be treated to a night of impressive astral views. Head to the Kielder Observatory if you'd like help identifying what you can see overhead.

65 EXMOOR DARK SKY DISCOVERY TRAIL

PARK AT: LAYBY ON
WELLSHEAD LANE
Exford,
Somerset
TA24 7NL
South West
*exmoorwalks.org/
darksky*

The whole of Exmoor National Park, away from big cities and light pollution, is a great place to spot constellations overhead, and this trail, marked with glow-in-the-dark signs, is an ace intro to the area. The 2-mile (3,2-kilometre) walk along an easy track begins beside a remote road and takes you onto moorland and over the ruins of Larkbarrow Farm. You might be tempted to bring a torch, but pick a clear night and the stars will light your way instead.

Surprising STONE CIRCLES

66 DUDDO FIVE STONES

ENTER VIA GATE
ON B5364 ROAD
Duddo,
Northumberland
TD15 2PT
North East

Five huge stones stand in a circle on a hill in a Northumberland farmer's field, braced against the wind and rain that has marked their surface for thousands of years. They've been standing here, forming a rough circle on a patch of land (now a handful of miles from the Scottish border), since the Bronze Age. Access is allowed along an unploughed path through farmland. Make your way along it and you're likely to have the place all to yourself at the end of your walk.

67 THE ROLLRIGHT STONES

Rollright Road
Little Rollright,
Oxfordshire
OX7 5QB
South East
rollrightstones.co.uk

In a quiet corner of the Cotswolds you'll find these relatively little-known stones. They are actually made up of three different monuments – a stone circle, a single standing stone, known as King Stone, and a burial chamber, called Whispering Knights – that were created at different times between 3800 and 1500 BC, from the early neolithic to the Bronze Age. The stone circle, known as the King's Men, was built around 2500 BC and still makes a neat, if weathered and slightly gappy, circle. It's a magical place to pause, and draws visitors a few times a year for low-key solstice and equinox celebrations.

68 AVEBURY STONE CIRCLE

Avebury,
Wiltshire
SN8 1RD
South West
+44 (0)16 7253 9250
nationaltrust.org.uk

Everyone's heard of Stonehenge but it's not England's only impressive stone circle. The circle at Avebury is on a different scale to the famous stones on the Salisbury Plain. It's the largest prehistoric stone circle on the planet, despite being far from the most famous. The stone circle and henge (circular earthwork), which was constructed between 2850 and 2200 BC, is also unusual in that it partially encloses Avebury village (and the village pub), which incredibly was built within the circle. There would have been around 100 stones originally, and though not all of them still stand, Avebury retains an atmospheric, otherworldly feel that continues to draw visitors, as well as pagans and the spiritually curious, year round. It's an entirely different experience to visiting Stonehenge, though. Here, you can wander freely and get as close as you like to the stones, as well as more neolithic monuments close by.

69 STANTON DREW STONE CIRCLE

Stanton Drew,
Somerset
BS39 4EW
South West
+44 (0)37 0333 1181
english-heritage.org.uk

Very few people would name Stanton Drew among England's collection of standing stones. Despite being the third largest standing stone site in the country and one that's considered historically significant, it's relatively unknown. Here there are three stone circles as well as a cove – thought to have been a site for ritual ceremonies, it's now, amazingly, in the garden of local pub The Druid's Arms – and you can get as close to them as you like. The largest of the stone circles, known as The Great Circle, has 26 imposing stones, still standing proudly on a floodplain.

70 CASTLERIGG STONE CIRCLE

Castle Lane
Underskiddaw,
Cumbria
CA12 4RN
North West
+44 (0)37 0333 1181
english-heritage.org.uk

In a remote spot outside Keswick, surrounded by incredible views of the Thirlmere Valley and the purple peaks of High Seat and Helvellyn, sits one of England's most atmospheric stone circles. Neolithic Castlerigg is both a stunning spot for soaking up ancient history and a peaceful place to appreciate the beauty of the Lakes.

71 MERRY MAIDENS

Next to B3315
Newlyn to
Treen Road
St Buryan,
Cornwall
TR19 6BQ
South West

The Merry Maidens are in a grassy field beside a rural road on the Penwith Peninsula, an area in Cornwall studded with megaliths and ancient ruins. Here there are 19 short stones in a circle, and coming across them, you get the sense you're the first person to have stumbled upon them for millenia. Despite being constructed well before Christianity reached England, legend has it that the Merry Maidens were women dancing at a wedding who were turned to stone as the evening turned into the next day, a Sunday. Two tall standing stones in fields nearby are known as The Pipers and were said to be the musicians accompanying them.

72 NINE LADIES STONE CIRCLE

AT: STANTON MOOR,
ACCESSED FROM
LEES ROAD
Stanton in Peak,
Derbyshire
DE4 2LS
Central England
+44 (0)16 2981 6200
english-heritage.org.uk

A small Bronze Age stone circle, made up of nine petite chunks of rock (ten, if you include one which has fallen), the Nine Ladies are in a quiet woodland clearing on the Peak District's atmospheric Stanton Moor. Visitors have left meaningful tokens in the centre of the circle, like crystals and shells. This is another circle said to depict a group of women who were turned to stone as punishment for dancing on a Sunday. The Nine Ladies are close to a number of other interesting sites. They are one of many prehistoric monuments dotted around Stanton Moor – begin your walk across the moor near Birchover to really soak up the historic space. About a 15-minute drive away, Arbor Law, is another huge neolithic monument on exposed moorland. Here you'll find 50 sizeable stones in a circle, and a central stone cove – a tight group of standing stones found within a larger circle – all of which have now fallen as well as a large earth bank and ditch.

73 GREY WETHERS CIRCLE

AT: DARTMOOR
NATIONAL PARK
Devon
PL20 6SZ
South West

There's something truly magical about finding Grey Wethers Circle, a double stone circle in the depths of Dartmoor National Park at the foot of Sittaford Tor. Both are formed of neat, uniform stones, low to the moorland. Thanks to the fact that accessing the stones means committing to a fairly long walk across Dartmoor, you'll likely have the intriguing spot all to yourself. Begin your trek at Fenworthy Reservoir and your route will also lead you past Fenworthy Stone Circle.

WILD SWIMMING *spots*

---

74 **LOWESWATER**
Cockermouth,
Cumbria
CA13 0RU
North West
+44 (0)15 3943 5599
nationaltrust.org.uk

If you like your wild swims with few spectators and zero chance of crossing paths with a motor boat, you'll love Loweswater, a lesser-known but incredibly picturesque body of water in the Lake District. The vibe here is quiet and peaceful. If you fancy stretching your legs once you've warmed up post-dip, there's a great circular walk around the lake. Look out for red squirrels and the Holme Force waterfall in the woods beside the water.

75 **HAMPSTEAD HEATH MIXED POND**
Hampstead
London
NW3 1BP
South East
cityoflondon.gov.uk

It's hardly a secret that there are wild swimming spots on London's Hampstead Heath, but that doesn't stop it feeling like one every time you slip into the deep water here. The natural bathing ponds are concealed by the trees, giving swimmers a sense that they've uncovered something incredibly special even on busy summer days. If you'd prefer not to share your swim, then opt for the Kenwood Ladies' or Highgate Men's ponds instead of the Mixed Pond, and consider taking the plunge out of season.

76 DIVER'S COVE

North Park Lane
Godstone,
Surrey
RH9 8ND
South East
diverscove.co.uk

Strong swimmers can make use of this 7.3-acre reservoir for an open air swim year round. It used to be a sand quarry which means the pond now has a soft sandy bottom. That and the stellar water quality mean it glows a turquoise shade in the sun. In winter, saunas and wood-fired hot tubs are available beside the water for warming up after a bracing dip.

77 BUDE SEA POOL

PARK AT: SUMMER-
LEAZE CAR PARK
Bude,
Cornwall
EX23 8HJ
South West
+44 (0)12 8848 8118
budeseapool.org

The halfway point between swimming in a lido and being thrown about by the Cornish waves, Bude Sea Pool is a semi-natural pool which was turned into a safe swim spot in the 1930s. The tidal pool is topped up with salty sea water (plus rocks, shells and sand) every high tide. It's just like sea swimming, but sheltered from the elements and the sea's currents. Best of all? It's totally free to use and run by a passionate team of volunteers.

75 HAMPSTEAD HEATH MIXED POND

78 GORMIRE LAKE

PARK AT: SUTTON BANK
VISITORS CENTRE
Near Thirsk,
North Yorkshire
YO7 2EH
North East

Gormire Lake is a pretty and peaceful spot for a swim, found at the base of Whitestone Cliff, surrounded by forest and the North York Moors National Park. It's a natural lake fed by an underground spring and some swimmers have even described Gormire as being warm, thanks to its lack of current or chilly streams feeding the lake.

79 CARDING MILL VALLEY RESERVOIR

Church Stretton,
Shropshire
SY6 6JG
Central England
+44 (0)16 9472 5000
nationaltrust.org.uk

In the beautiful Shropshire Hills, Carding Mill Valley is a wildlife and history rich area, with lush views and great walking routes. It's also the ideal place for an alfresco splash. The area's reservoir, now decommissioned, is a sheltered and secluded place for a wild swim. It's also just a short walk to the National Trust-run tearoom if you need a little help warming up afterwards.

80 MONSAL DALE WEIR

Monsal Head,
Derbyshire
DE45 1NL
Central England

Monsal Dale Weir is a mega place for a wild dip right in the heart of the Peak District. Not only is the spot stunning, so is the walk down to it from Monsal Head. The route takes in views of Monsal Dale, Headstone Viaduct and the River Wye. Just below the weir is the perfect place for a paddle or a full on plunge if you're brave.

81 PORT MEADOW

Walton Well Road
Oxford,
Oxfordshire
OX2 6ED
South East

One of Oxford's largest and loveliest open spaces, Port Meadow is a big swathe of green scored by the River Thames and its tributaries. The meadow has long drawn those looking for an alfresco swim, as well as paddleboarders and rowers, and it's recently been designated an official river bathing spot. That means the water quality is regularly tested – and the results displayed – in the summer months to make sure it's safe. Good news all round.

82 GRANTCHESTER MEADOWS

Cambridge,
Cambridgeshire
CB3 9ED
East of England

The broad meadows that edge the River Cam to the south of the city of Cambridge have long been a popular spot for picnicking, wild swimming and messing about on punts. The river might be busy with visiting tourists on summer days, but the sheer size of the floodplain meadows mean you can always find a patch of riverbank all to yourself.

83 SHILLEY POOL

AT: DARTMOOR
NATIONAL PARK
Devon
EX20 2QF
South West

A secluded swimming spot on Dartmoor, Shilley Pool is a natural rock pool filled by Blackaton Brook. A section of stone has been beautifully flattened by the stream over the centuries, making a perfectly smooth natural slide into the pool below. Discover it by taking a brisk uphill walk along the south side of the brook from the narrow road between South Zeal and Throwleigh.

Ancient **HISTORY**

84 WEST KENNET LONG BARROW

West Kennett,
Wiltshire
SN8 1QH
South West
+44 (0)16 7253 9250
english-heritage.org.uk

Pull into a layby by the side of the A4 and take a short walk away from the road to find West Kennet Long Barrow, one of the largest and most accessible neolithic tombs in England. The impressive burial chamber was constructed around 3650 BC and became the final resting place for around 50 people. Huge stones mark the ancient tomb's entrance, and visitors are free to wander inside the sacred space. It's an incredible, atmospheric place.

85 HALLIGGYE FOGOU

AT: TRELOWARREN
ESTATE
Mawgan,
Cornwall
TR12 6AF
South West
+44 (0)37 0333 1181
english-heritage.org.uk

Fogou, from the Cornish word meaning cave, is used to name a few mysterious man-made underground spaces that date from the Cornish Iron Age, around the 4th or 5th century BC. The purpose of the underground passages and tunnels remains unknown, though theories range from shrines and storage spaces to refuges for the farming communities who built them. Halliggye Fogou is the best-preserved example, intact enough that visitors can step down inside and explore the unusual passage itself.

86 RICHBOROUGH ROMAN FORT

Off Richborough
Road
Sandwich,
Kent
CT13 9JW
South East
+44 (0)37 0333 1181
english-heritage.org.uk

An unassuming spot near the coast and the pretty village of Sandwich, Richborough Roman Fort is actually one of the most important Roman sites in the entire country. Parts of the enormous, now crumbling, walls of a Roman fort still stand alongside stone foundations and impressive defensive earthworks, while the remains of a large amphitheatre are also a short walk away. Richborough doesn't sit right on the coast now, but it would have done 2000 years ago. What was the first place the Romans stepped foot on English soil later became a thriving port town and then later still an enormous defensive fort – the area was in use throughout the entire Roman occupation, from 23 AD to around 410 AD. Check out the foundations of one of the empire's biggest monumental arches. Built in 85 AD, the elaborate arch acted as a literal gateway to Roman Britannia.

87 HARDKNOTT ROMAN FORT

Hardknott Pass
Eskdale,
Cumbria
CA19 1TH
North West
+44 (0)37 0333 1181
english-heritage.org.uk

Ruins don't get much more dramatic than Hardknott Roman Fort. The fort, which was built early in the 2nd century during Emperor Hadrian's rule, is really remote, situated above the Esk Valley in a bleak stretch of the Lake District. The stone foundations of the fort, headquarters, a commandant's house and a bath house remain, and are free to explore at any time. It's accessed via Hardknott Pass, a steep hill pass, which is fairly treacherous in bad weather.

88 BARTLOW HILLS

Bartlow,
Cambridgeshire
CB21 4EN
East of England

The significance of this group of man-made mounds on the outskirts of Bartlow village could easily be missed. Largely unknown and now a little overgrown, the mounds, four of which remain intact, are actually Roman burial mounds, built around the 1st or 2nd century. Three of the tumuli are accessible to the public, and the tallest can be climbed via a steep set of wooden stairs for a unique view over this incredible site.

89 WROXETER ROMAN CITY

Wroxeter,
Shropshire
SY5 6PH
Central England
+44 (0)17 4376 1330
english-heritage.org.uk

Never heard of Wroxeter? Founded in the 1st century, Wroxeter (or *Viroconium*) was once one of the largest cities in Roman Britain, and it's estimated that it was as big as Italy's famous Pompeii. It's thought the Romans moved into land that had already been inhabited during the Iron Age, if not for centuries before, building a fortress and later a town, with baths and a forum. Its rural location means the ground hasn't been disturbed much over the centuries, so the remains that have been excavated are incredibly well preserved. What's most incredible of all is to look around you knowing that most of the Roman town still remains buried beneath the grass.

90 CHESTER CITY WALLS

Chester,
Cheshire
CH1 1QX
North West

You've heard of Hadrian's Wall, the incredible 73-mile (117-kilometre) Roman wall built to guard the northern reaches of the Roman Empire (huge stretches of this wall still stand, along with incredible ruins like the most complete example of a Roman fort at Housesteads), but have you heard of Chester's Roman walls? Chester is the only city in England that is still completely encircled by its ancient defensive walls. They've been standing for around 2000 years, though were partially rebuilt in the 12th century, and you can still take a walk around them today.

DE LA WARR PAVILION

BUILDINGS

MODERNIST *architecture*

91 THE HOMEWOOD

Portsmouth Road
Esher,
Surrey
KT10 9JL
South East
+44 (0)13 7246 7806
nationaltrust.org.uk

A modernist masterpiece, completed in 1938 and designed by the architect Patrick Gwynne, The Homewood is a family home turned museum piece. With its concrete frame, enormous windows and open plan design, it's a captivating example of modernist architecture. The home, which Gwynne lived in until his death in 2003, sits among the trees at the top of a gently sloping and expansive garden, which is also well worth an explore during a visit. Tours take place just once a week between April and October.

92 DE LA WARR PAVILION

Marina
Bexhill-On-Sea,
East Sussex
TN40 1DP
South East
+44 (0)14 2422 9111
dlwp.com

Built in 1935, this Grade I-listed beachfront pavilion is an art deco delight, and beloved local landmark. Coastal light streams in through curved glass windows and down swirling internal staircases, while epic views of the sea are framed by neat balconies. The building is open seven days a week and is free to enter (as are any art exhibitions taking place), though the De La Warr Pavilion also hosts a number of ticketed events, like comedy and musical performances, thought-provoking get-togethers and workshops.

93 2 WILLOW ROAD

Hampstead,
London
NW3 1TH
South East
+44 (0)20 7435 6166
nationaltrust.org.uk

Completed in 1939, 2 Willow Road is the former home of architect Ernö Goldfinger, who designed London's iconic brutalist tower block Trellick Tower among others. Goldfinger's spacious and thoughtfully composed home remains as he designed it, complete with his collection of modernist furniture and his impressive art collection. It is now a much-loved building, despite not going down well with locals, who didn't think it fitted in with the character of the Hampstead neighbourhood, at the time. Visits are by pre-booked guided tour only.

92 DE LA WARR PAVILION

Remarkable RUINS

94 **SUTTON SCARSDALE HALL**

Hall Drive
Sutton Scarsdale,
Derbyshire
S44 5UR
Central England
+44 (0)37 0333 1181
english-heritage.org.uk

A baroque-style masterpiece, complete with a decorative, hand-carved stone exterior and stunning stucco decoration inside, Sutton Scarsdale Hall was built in the 1720s for the 4th Earl of Scarsdale. The Scarsdales sold it to a local family in the 19th century, and when they in turn were forced to sell it in 1919, the hall ended up in the hands of asset strippers, who sold its interiors and reduced the once grand home to a roofless shell. Amazingly three of the rooms still exist and are on display at the Museum of Art in Philadelphia, while a pine-panelled room is at the Huntington Library in California. The hall is now a preserved set of unique ruins, a skeleton of a country house sat high on a hill.

95 CLUN CASTLE

Clun,
Shropshire
SY7 8JT
Central England
+44 (0)37 0333 1181
english-heritage.org.uk

Set on a steep hill looking down on the tiny town of Clun, Clun Castle was built in the 11th century as a demonstration of the English monarchy's power in this region. The castle and the town that grew to surround it saw prosperous times, as well as numerous attacks from across the Welsh border, just a few miles to the town's west. Now all that remains are impressive earthworks and a grand crumbling tower, where glimpses of the lush Shropshire countryside can be seen through the gaping, wildflower-adorned windows.

96 RIEVAULX ABBEY

Rievaulx,
North Yorkshire
YO62 5LB
North East
+44 (0)14 3979 8228
english-heritage.org.uk

Hidden away in a peaceful valley beside the River Rye, you'll discover the otherworldly ruins of Rievaulx Abbey – all graceful arches and grand glassless windows surrounded by greenery. The impressive Cistercian abbey was founded in the 12th century, before being shut down and dismantled in 1538 as part of King Henry VIII's suppression of the monasteries. Yorkshire's countryside is dotted with the ruins of abbeys and monasteries with similar histories. Two of the most well-known are Fountains Abbey, an internationally recognised World Heritage Site on the edge of the Yorkshire Dales, and Whitby Abbey, the Gothic, clifftop masterpiece which sits above the town and was famously an inspiration for Bram Stoker's *Dracula*.

97 DONNINGTON CASTLE

Donnington,
Berkshire
RG14 2LE
South East
+44 (0)37 0333 1181
english-heritage.org.uk

Walking up the hill to find the solitary ruins of Donnington Castle – a castle which is thought to have hosted both Henry VIII and Elizabeth I before being badly damaged during the English Civil War – you get a sense that it's being discovered for the first time. The ruins, a proud two-towered gatehouse alongside low walls that reveal the castle's original layout, sit in a rural spot surveying the outskirts of Newbury. Look up at the back wall of the gatehouse, which is dotted with fireplaces and doorways, showing where different floor levels would have once been.

98 WHEAL COATES

Beacon Drive
St Agnes,
Cornwall
TR5 0NT
South West
+44 (0)18 7255 2412
nationaltrust.org.uk

On an isolated Cornish headland with mega views of the Atlantic Ocean, you'll find Wheal Coates. These are dramatic clifftop ruins, but not the kind you might imagine. A Unesco World Heritage Site, Wheal Coates is a collection of ruined tin mining buildings that hark back to Cornwall's industrial past. Visitors can walk in the footsteps of the miners who worked here in the 19th century in this bleak yet beautiful spot.

99 MORETON CORBET CASTLE

Moreton Corbet,
Shropshire
SY4 4DW
Central England
+44 (0)37 0333 1181
english-heritage.org.uk

There's something incredibly surreal about the remains of Moreton Corbet Castle. Grand Italianate windows that have long lost their glass and intricate brickwork, which dates from the Elizabethan era, now sit alongside the corrugated iron of farm buildings, overlooking agricultural fields. There's no grand entrance, just a small layby for visitors to park in. The unusual ruins create wonderful shadows on the surrounding grass on a sunny day.

100 BODIAM CASTLE

Bodiam,
East Sussex
TN32 5UA
South East
+44 (0)15 8083 0196
nationaltrust.org.uk

Built in 1385 as a grand home for knight and royal favourite Sir Edward Dallingridge and his wife Elizabeth, Bodiam Castle is a picture-perfect castle, complete with glassy moat, battlements, neat lookout towers and thin windows you can imagine an arrow flying right out of. From outside it appears perfectly preserved – even the castle's original wooden portcullis still resides in the gatehouse. Inside those great 14th-century walls, though, Bodiam is largely ruined, with just a few rooms and some wall foundations still standing.

101 DUNSTANBURGH CASTLE

Dunstanburgh Road
Craster,
Northumberland
NE66 3TT
North East
+44 (0)16 6557 6231
english-heritage.org.uk

Isolated, remote and battered by the elements, the ruins of huge Dunstanburgh Castle – the largest in Northumberland – stand beside the North Sea. The coastal fortress was built in the 14th century, though it's believed the exposed headland the dramatic ruins now stand on was inhabited for thousands of years before that. The view of the castle's twin-towered keep from the south is especially stunning. You'll see it as you take the 1,3-mile (2-kilometre) walk to reach the relic from the closest car park in nearby Craster village.

102 WOLVESEY CASTLE

College St
Winchester,
Hampshire
SO23 9NB
South East
+44 (0)37 0333 1181
english-heritage.org.uk

It's easy to walk straight past the unassuming entrance to these impressive ruins, tucked away behind Winchester's famous Cathedral, between The Pilgrim's School and their playing fields. The narrow pathway opens up to reveal surprisingly extensive ruins of what was once the grand residence of the wealthy and powerful Medieval Bishops of Winchester, a space which hosted Queen Mary and Philip of Spain's wedding banquet in 1554. The 12th-century palace is now mainly low-level walls and foundations with some archways and towers remaining standing. It's an atmospheric place that, thanks to its easily missable entrance, you could have all to yourself.

103 WAVERLEY ABBEY

Waverley Lane
Farnham,
Surrey
GU9 8EP
South East
+44 (0)37 0333 1181
english-heritage.org.uk

In a peaceful spot beside the River Wey, this was the very first monastery founded in England by the Cistercian religious order after a small group of French monks settled here in 1128. What you can see today are the evocative remains of a once very active monastery, some parts of which are still standing strong. The most impressive section is the former lay brothers' quarters where delicate columns still support the vaulted ceiling above. Look out too for an ancient yew tree, whose roots are growing in and around the ruins, which is thought to be more than 500 years old.

Ancient CHURCHES

104 GREENSTED CHURCH

Church Lane
Ongar,
Essex
CM5 9LD
East of England
+44 (0)78 8495 9619
greensted church.org.uk

A tiny place of worship in a rural corner of Essex, Greensted Church is actually the oldest wooden church on the planet. Amazingly, the 51 timber planks in the nave that you can still see today date from around 1060, although excavations have revealed two even earlier wooden structures from the 6th and 7th centuries on the site. Other parts of the church, like the wood clad tower, were added between the 15th and 17th centuries. The Grade I-listed building remains a working church with regular services, while the doors are usually open for visitors to have a look inside.

105 ST MARTIN'S CHURCH

North Holmes Road
Canterbury,
Kent
CT1 1PW
South East
+44 (0)12 2776 8072
martinpaul.org

Part of Canterbury's protected Unesco World Heritage Site, St Martin's Church is considered to be the oldest church in England. The building was used as a place of worship by Christian Queen Bertha from 580 AD, during her marriage to Pagan Ethelbert of Kent – and the church has been in continuous use as a place of worship since then. The structure you see today incorporates Roman and Anglo-Saxon design as well as later additions. Despite its modest appearance, this unassuming parish church is considered to be as historically important as grand Canterbury Cathedral itself.

106 ESCOMB SAXON CHURCH

Escomb Green
Escomb,
County Durham
DL14 7SW
North East
+44 (0)13 8860 2860

Founded in the 670s, this is considered to be the oldest complete Saxon church in England. It certainly looks and feels like a relic from another time. Inside, you'll find simple whitewashed walls and plain wooden pews. The uneven brickwork on the church's external walls is thought to be a result of the building being constructed out of repurposed Roman stone from a nearby fort.

Incredible **MANOR HOUSES**

107 OXBURGH HALL

Oxborough,
Norfolk
PE33 9PS
East of England
+44 (0)13 6632 8258
nationaltrust.org.uk

Oxburgh's beautiful red brick exterior is perfectly reflected in its neat accompanying moat. A 15th-century family home of epic proportions, Oxburgh Hall has had periods of near dereliction and was even threatened with demolition, but thankfully the dreamy manor was saved and is now preserved for future generations. The tranquil spot, complete with formal gardens, meadow and woodland, feels like a retreat from the real world.

108 GAWTHORPE HALL

Burnley Road
Padiham,
Lancashire
BB12 8UA
North West
+44 (0)12 8277 1004
nationaltrust.org.uk

You might be familiar with two other buildings designed by Sir Charles Barry, who redesigned Gawthorpe Hall in the 1850s. Barry was responsible for the Houses of Parliament as well as Highclere Castle, the Berkshire pile which has become famous as the setting for *Downton Abbey*. In fact, Gawthorpe is sometimes now referred to as the 'Downton of the North'. Visit to explore the house, which often hosts exhibitions, take in the estate's pretty grounds or, if you're a big reader, soak up the house's Brontë connection. A stop off on the Brontë Way walking route, which runs from Lancashire to West Yorkshire, Gawthorpe Hall is somewhere Charlotte Brontë is known to have visited.

109 CALKE ABBEY

Ticknall,
Derbyshire
DE73 7JF
Central England
+44 (0)13 3286 3822
nationaltrust.org.uk

The National Trust, who look after this crumbling manor house, have affectionately dubbed it the 'un-stately' home. Why? Because it's frozen in time, preserved as it was when the Trust started caring for it in 1985. Instead of grand rooms, filled with gleaming historical objects neatly arranged to illustrate the building's prime, such as you see in most of England's great manor houses, Calke has remained as it was when its final private owners gave it away – in decline, with abandoned rooms, peeling wallpaper, dust and all. It makes an unusual but fascinating place to explore, where the sense of what once was is even more palpable.

110 ICKWORTH

Horringer,
Suffolk
IP29 5QE
East of England
+44 (0)12 8473 5270
nationaltrust.org.uk

Suffolk isn't exactly the place you'd expect to find a grand Italian-style villa. Yet here one stands, built in the late 18th century to replace an older and less fashionable manor on the estate. The stand-out feature is its bold rotunda, designed to be a space to show off the 4th Earl of Bristol's impressive collections from his travels around Europe. Incredibly the building's west wing was added only for the aesthetic symmetry and remained an empty shell until the National Trust turned it into their visitor centre. The east wing is now part of the Luxury Family Hotels group.

111 PETWORTH HOUSE AND PARK

Petworth,
West Sussex
GU28 9LR
South East
+44 (0)17 9834 2207
nationaltrust.org.uk

One enormous manor house, Petworth is an imposing stone construction filled with famous works of art, gilded reception rooms and meticulously reconstructed servants' quarters. The real star though is what the house looks out over: 700 acres of glorious deer park, dotted with ancient trees and around 800 deer, who you can spot if you head to the park's quieter further reaches.

Fairytale **FOLLIES**

112 **HACKFALL**

Near Grewelthorpe,
North Yorkshire
HG4 3BS
North East
woodlandtrust.org.uk

Now a seemingly wild stretch of forest in the
care of the Woodland Trust, Hackfall was once
a meticulously designed ornamental landscape,
created by landowner William Aislabie in the
18th century. Aislabie planted trees, created water
features and designed and built a number of follies
that are concealed within the woodland. All of
his wooden buildings have since disappeared,
while other stone constructions have been ruined
over time, but there are still some wonderful
structures to be found here. Now standing without
its original roof or windows, circular Fisher's Hall
is a surreal sight to stumble upon in the middle of
the woodland. Visitors can spot the mock ruins of
miniature Mowbray Castle between the leaves and
the Rustic Temple beside a lake. One of Aislabie's
follies, the Grade II*-listed banqueting house,
known as The Ruin, has been fully restored by
the Landmark Trust and can now be rented for
overnight stays.

113 STOURHEAD

Near Mere,
Wiltshire
BA12 6QD
South West
+44 (0)17 4784 1152
nationaltrust.org.uk

There's a grand Palladian-style villa at Stourhead, but if you head deeper into the estate's stunning, landscaped garden you'll stumble upon a number of even more captivating buildings. Wandering around Stourhead's glassy lake, you'll come across the tiny Temple of Flora, a cool, cave-like grotto, and the Pantheon, a grand structure inspired by Rome's Pantheon that sits right at the water's edge. Elsewhere, more follies appear. Don't miss the Temple of Apollo, an intriguing circular structure with amazing views over the lake.

114 STOWE GARDENS

Buckingham,
Buckinghamshire
MK18 5EQ
South East
+44 (0)12 8081 7156
nationaltrust.org.uk

The enormous expanse of land at Stowe is dotted with follies, temples, monuments and grottoes designed to enthral the 18th-century gentry. Though some features of Lord Cobham's ambitious gardens have been lost, there are 250 acres of Grade I-listed garden and 1000 acres of parkland to explore today, packed with a huge number of garden buildings, like the incredible Gothic Temple and the Temple of Friendship. Wander wherever your curiosity takes you.

116 CLAIFE VIEWING STATION

115 FARINGDON FOLLY TOWER AND WOODLAND

Stanford Road
Faringdon,
Oxfordshire
SN7 8EP
South East
*faringdon
folly.org.uk*

Built in 1935 by Lord Berners, this tower was granted planning permission on the condition that it could only be a little higher than the surrounding trees, so although it boasts impressive views of the surrounding countryside, it's almost imperceptible from many angles when the leaves are fully out. A true folly, the 100-foot (30,5-metre) tower was built with no intention of ever having a use, though you can now rent the room at the top of the tower for private events. Look out for wooden sculptures and carvings in the trees that surround the tower.

116 CLAIFE VIEWING STATION

Beside the ferry
on Windermere's
west shore
Near Far Sawrey,
Hawkshead,
Cumbria
North West
+44 (0)15 3944 1456
nationaltrust.org.uk

Built in the 1790s, this stone construction, which looks a little like the ruins of a tiny castle, was actually built as a place from which early tourists could admire the views of Lake Windermere. It was even used as a location for dances in the early 19th century, when each of the windows were set with a different shade of coloured glass to give the viewer a sense of seeing the lake in different seasons and weather conditions. It's been partially restored and is now open to the elements, but it is still a dreamy place to take in your surroundings.

Beautiful
NEW CONSTRUCTIONS

117 FIRST LIGHT PAVILION

AT: JODRELL BANK
Bomish Lane
Lower Withington,
Cheshire
SK11 9DL
North West
+44 (0)14 7757 1766
jodrellbank.net

The newest addition to Jodrell Bank Observatory – itself a Unesco World Heritage Site – is the First Light Pavilion, an enormous, grass-topped concrete dome, which is designed to echo the shape and scale of the iconic Lovell Telescope (a radio telescope at Jodrell Bank). It contains exhibition space as well as a custom-built 'space dome' auditorium, but the building is also pretty cool for another reason. First Light Pavilion aligns with the sun. The sun shines in through a slim window right in the centre of the building and moves across the entrance foyer as the day goes on, like a giant sundial.

118 THE HEPWORTH WAKEFIELD

Gallery Walk
Wakefield,
West Yorkshire
WF1 5AW
North East
+44 (0)19 2424 7360
*hepworth
wakefield.org*

Opened in 2011, the Hepworth Wakefield is a beautiful new waterside home for the work of Barbara Hepworth, Henry Moore and other 20th-century artists. Skylights and huge windows flood the gallery with light, while its angular design is intended to mirror the shapes found in Hepworth's much-loved sculptures. Make time to also explore the Hepworth Wakefield Garden, a free, flower-filled public space next to the gallery.

119 HASTINGS PIER

White Rock
Hastings,
East Sussex
TN34 1JY
South East

After Hastings' original pier was destroyed by fire in 2010, a new and incredibly lovely to look at pier by dRMM architects was built in its place, which reopened in 2016. Hastings Pier, which has picked up a number of architectural awards for its sleek and simplistic design, is now a wide open space with uninterrupted views of the waves. There are beach huts selling drinks and snacks, while open-air musical performances fill the space during the summer months.

120 WINDERMERE JETTY MUSEUM

Rayrigg Road
Windermere,
Cumbria
LA23 1BN
North West
+44 (0)15 3963 7940
lakelandarts.org.uk

The first new building to be constructed on the shores of Lake Windermere for quite a while, the Windermere Jetty Museum, which opened in 2019, is all sleek lines and neat shapes. It manages to be both bold in design and sensitive to its stunning Lake District surroundings. The connected buildings, which tell the story of sailing on the lake from the 18th century to today, do an ace job of framing and showcasing stellar views of the water.

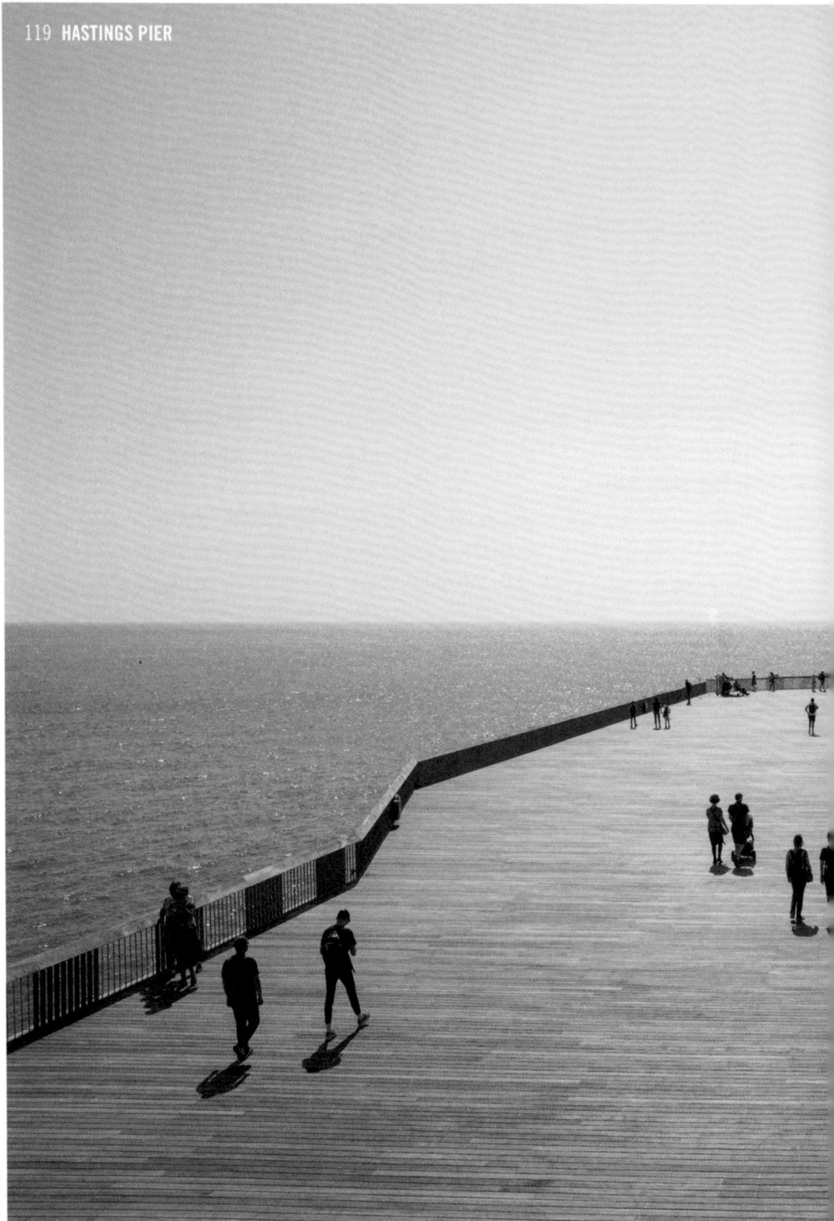
119 **HASTINGS PIER**

MEDIEVAL and TUDOR
buildings

121 173 HIGH STREET

Berkhamsted,
Hertfordshire
HP4 3HB
East of England

Plenty of people must walk straight past this estate agent everyday without knowing its significance. Hidden in plain sight, number 173 on Berkhamsted's high street has been called the oldest shop in England, and it's certainly one of the oldest jettied timber-framed buildings still standing. Incredibly, the building dates back to the 13th century, sometime between 1277 and 1297. Its impressive history was only discovered in 2001 when the age of the building's timber was analysed during renovations.

122 MARKET HALL

High St
Chipping Campden,
Gloucestershire
GL55 6AJ
South West
+44 (0)13 8643 8333
nationaltrust.org.uk

This honey-hued market hall, built out of creamy Cotswold stone 400 years ago, still stands in the centre of Chipping Campden. It was designed as a shelter for local traders hawking their wares. A lot has changed in the town since its construction, but the beautiful building, and its stone floor worn smooth over the centuries, still evokes a sense of how the town must have felt during the 17th century.

123 LAVENHAM GUILDHALL

Market Place
Lavenham,
Suffolk
CO10 9QZ
East of England
+44 (0)17 8724 7646
nationaltrust.org.uk

Arguably Lavenham's most impressive medieval building, the Guildhall (also known as the Guildhall of Corpus Christi) is a beautiful timber-framed construction in shades of white and grey. It was built in around 1530 and still looks much as it would have done then, despite a colourful history – the Guildhall has been a prison, a workhouse, a pub, a chapel and a social club for US troops during WWII. Visitors can wander around inside what is now a museum and tearoom.

124 LITTLE MORETON HALL

Newcastle Road
Congleton,
Cheshire
CW12 4SD
North West
+44 (0)12 6027 2018
nationaltrust.org.uk

A trippy timber-framed Tudor manor house, Little Moreton Hall is more than a little wonky. Despite subsidence, in part due to its top-heavy design, it's still stable and standing, more than 500 years since it was built. You can admire the Grade I-listed building's intricate monochrome design and incredibly well-preserved interiors, as well as its accompanying moat, on the handful of days it's open to the public each month.

125 GAINSBOROUGH OLD HALL

Parnell St
Gainsborough,
Lincolnshire
DN21 2NB
Central England
+44 (0)14 2767 7348
english-heritage.org.uk

A medieval manor house built in the late 15th century, little-known Gainsborough Old Hall has had a varied history. Starting life as the grand seat of the Burgh family, it was separated over the years, the building having had turns as a workshop, linen factory, tenements, a theatre, assembly rooms, the headquarters of a literary institute and a Masonic lodge. It remains one of the finest medieval manors in the country. Check out the Great Hall's original timber ceiling and the impressively well-preserved kitchen with its huge fireplace.

Impressive CASTLES

126 CASTLE DROGO

Drewsteignton,
Devon
EX6 6PB
South West
+44 (0)16 4743 3306
nationaltrust.org.uk

Constructed between 1911 and 1930, Castle Drogo was the last castle to be built in England. It was designed by architect Sir Edwin Lutyens for Julius Drewe, a businessman who sadly died the year after construction was completed, and the castle stayed in the Drewe family until it was gifted to the National Trust in 1974. The bold construction, built out of huge granite blocks, looks out over the Teign Gorge surrounded by Dartmoor's craggy tors. It's a stunning spot for a castle – the views out of the windows are as arresting as the grand 1920s-style interiors – and a great starting point for a walk through the surrounding area.

127 BERKELEY CASTLE

Berkeley,
Gloucestershire
GL13 9BQ
South West
+44 (0)14 5381 0303
berkeley-castle.com

Incredibly, this castle, sat between the Cotswolds and the River Severn, has been home to the Berkeley family for nine entire centuries. It is the oldest building in the country to still be inhabited by the family who built it. Built for conflict, it was completed in the 12th century as a fortress to protect England's border with Wales, but has also very much been a family home and visitors will find many intriguing treasures collected by the Berkeleys over the years, like a bedspread once used by Queen Elizabeth I.

128 ARUNDEL CASTLE

Arundel,
West Sussex
BN18 9AB
South East
+44 (0)19 0388 2173
arundelcastle.org

A fairytale-esque, intact castle overlooking the town of Arundel and the River Arun, this impressive fortress dates back nearly a millennium. The motte, gatehouse and dry moat were built around 1070, while the rest of the castle has grown and been added to in the intervening years. When the castle and its gardens are open to the public (usually from April to the end of October), you can tour the moat, browse the shelves in the library, peer into grand bedrooms and enjoy views from the 11th-century keep.

129 ORFORD CASTLE

Orford,
Suffolk
IP12 2ND
East of England
+44 (0)13 9445 0472
english-heritage.org.uk

Built in the 12th century under orders from King Henry II, this coastal castle was once a symbol of royal power in the region. Just the keep, a polygonal tower, still stands, surrounded by earthworks which reveal where further walls would have once been. But the keep remains intact, and incredibly well preserved. Visitors can explore all the rooms, from the castle's basement through to its roof, which boasts views of Orford Ness Nature Reserve and the sea beyond.

LAVENHAM

PLACES 🔑

Chocolate box **VILLAGES**

130 **LAVENHAM**
Suffolk
East of England

A small village surrounded by Suffolk countryside, Lavenham has more than its fair share of medieval charm. It was once a prosperous wool town and the historic evidence remains: everywhere you turn there are pretty and perfectly preserved half-timbered houses and pastel-painted cottages. More than 300 of the village's buildings are listed. The tangle of narrow streets, which centre around Lavenham's ancient Market Place, is an ace spot for an atmospheric wander and a pitstop in a traditional tearoom. Don't miss the Guildhall, The Crooked House or De Vere House, a beautiful building which appears in the *Harry Potter* movies (and is available to rent on Airbnb.)

131 **CASTLETON**
Derbyshire
Central England

This pretty village in the Peaks has it all: a ruined Norman castle, cute cafes, welcoming pubs and neat stone cottages, all in the shadow of Mam Tor (also evocatively known as Shivering Mountain), a stunning nearby peak. Don't miss Peak Cavern, the entrance to an epic cave system, on the outskirts of town.

132 LACOCK

Wiltshire
South West
nationaltrust.org.uk

Walking around Lacock feels like stepping on to the set of a period drama, and for good reason: it's starred in countless films and TV dramas. The village, which is so well preserved it's almost entirely owned by the National Trust, is a total time warp, with no TV aerials or electricity cables in sight. Stop by the 800-year-old, honey-hued abbey before checking out the bakery or settling down in one of the village's traditional pubs. A number of locals sell handmade trinkets from their doorsteps – pay by dropping the money through their letterboxes.

133 ALFRISTON

East Sussex
South East
alfriston-village.co.uk

Tiny Alfriston is pretty as a postcard. Its narrow streets are stuffed full of lovely looking historic buildings. Discover independent shops, traditional tearooms and welcoming pubs, plus an expansive village green. Stick around to visit nearby Seaford Head Nature Reserve and Cuckmere Haven, which offer dreamy views of the Seven Sisters chalk cliffs.

134 STAITHES

North Yorkshire
North East

18th-century fishing cottages cling to the shoreline in Staithes, a stunning coastal village just north of gothic Whitby (also well worth a visit, though the town, with its haunted clifftop ruins, is far too famous to be called hidden!) Staithes used to be one of the largest fishing ports in the North East, but it's quieter these days. There's still fresh fish and seafood to be found at the harbour, as well as tearooms and art galleries along the village's cobbled streets.

135 CLOVELLY

Devon
South West
clovelly.co.uk

You'll find steep hills, cobbled streets and zero cars in Clovelly, an incredibly picturesque fishing village in Devon. Visitors must leave their cars at the entrance to the village before venturing downhill towards the harbour on foot – even locals use sledges to move deliveries and shopping around the village. Clovelly is privately owned so expect to pay an entrance fee, which goes towards maintaining and restoring the ancient village and its unique, old-world vibes.

136 MILTON ABBAS

Dorset
South West

This unusual, and very photogenic, village was actually designed by architect William Chambers and renowned landscape gardener Capability Brown in the 1770s, making it one of the first planned settlements in England. Running through a lush wooded valley, Milton Abbas's The Street is lined by almost identical white thatched cottages.

137 GREAT BUDWORTH

Cheshire
North West
greatbudworth.com

A tiny village populated with neat brown brick and half-timbered cottages, Great Budworth is so ancient it was recorded in the *Domesday Book* of 1086. Cobbled walkways and a 14th-century church at the village's heart add to the feeling that you've fallen back through time.

138 DOWNHAM

Lancashire
North West
*downham
village.org.uk*

There are no overhead wires, satellite dishes or TV aerials in Downham, giving a surreal impression that the well-preserved village, which is dotted with listed buildings, never moved into the 21st century. Visit to admire the mix of grand and humble homes which look the same today as they did hundreds of years ago. You'll also find a tearoom, pub and village shop, plus many walking routes out into the surrounding Forest of Bowland countryside.

139 HEPTONSTALL

West Yorkshire
North East

Sat high on a hill above Hebden Bridge, Heptonstall is a proper hidden gem. It used to be a hand-loom weaving hub, so you'll notice many of the cottages have large first floor windows to let in extra daylight. One of the oldest villages in Yorkshire, quiet Heptonstall boasts plenty of ancient features. Residents successfully campaigned for the villages' original cobblestones to be revealed and Victorian gas lamps to be returned, replacing standard electric street lighting, in the 1980s. Writer Sylvia Plath is buried in the village's graveyard, while the atmospheric ruins of the Church of St Thomas à Becket are absolutely worth a visit.

A B A N D O N E D *towns*

140 **GAINSTHORPE MEDIEVAL VILLAGE**

Gainsthorpe Road
East and West
Kirton in Lindsey,
Lincolnshire
DN21 4JH
Central England
+44 (0)37 0333 1181
english-heritage.org.uk

What was once a small medieval farming village with a chapel and a windmill is now a series of atmospheric bumps, ridges and hollows in a fascinating unploughed field. Amazingly, many elements of Gainsthorpe still remain, including the outlines of barns, houses, dovecotes and even village streets in the grassy landscape. The village was actually deserted by 1616, though no records reveal how or why the villagers disappeared.

141 **HALLSANDS**

Devon
South West

Walk the South West Coast Path between Start Point and Beesands to get a sense of what happened at Hallsands, a small fishing village that has been almost entirely been swallowed by the sea. A huge storm in 1917 washed away homes, a village store and the village pub – an entire community – leaving just one house standing. You can see the ruins of the village from the viewing platform on the cliff edge. The disaster was caused by dredging, which destabilised the coastline, but, in the context of our ongoing climate emergency, it makes for a thought-provoking stop.

142 WHARRAM PERCY

Centenary Way
Wharram-le-Street,
North Yorkshire
YO17 9TD
North East
+44 (0)37 0333 1181
english-heritage.org.uk

A rural village, occupied for around 600 years before it was deserted, the remains of medieval Wharram Percy are clear to see. Access is by foot, and the village is nearly a mile (1,6 kilometre) from the car park. Those who make the trek can wander past the atmospheric remains of the ancient village church, pause by the village pond, and discover the grassed-over foundations of a vicarage, manor houses, peasants' homes, barns and outbuildings in the surrounding greenery.

143 IMBER

Wiltshire
South West
imbervillage.co.uk

All the residents of Imber village on the Salisbury Plain were issued with eviction notices in 1943, during World War II. Incredibly, they were given just 47 days' notice to leave their homes, as the village and surrounding land was set to become a training ground for American troops. Despite protests from the community, the village was never handed back and remains a training ground to this day. Many of Imber's historic buildings have been demolished, but The Ministry of Defence do allow public access on a handful of days a year, where visitors can step inside St Giles' Church and wander around the surreal remains of the village.

144 CHYSAUSTER ANCIENT VILLAGE

New Mill,
Cornwall
TR20 8XA
South West
+44 (0)37 0333 1181
english-heritage.org.uk

In the rural wilds of Cornwall's Penwith peninsula, this ancient but amazingly well-preserved village comes as a surprise when it appears at the top of the hill. A peaceful location with sea views, it's easy to see why a community would have wanted to call this spot home. Parts of the stone walls of this Iron Age village still stand, with clear rooms and doorways, set along a village street. You can step inside the unusual courtyard-style houses, which are only seen in this area of mainland Cornwall and the Scilly Isles.

Lovely **L I D O S** *and outdoor* **P O O L S**

145 **JUBILEE POOL**

Battery Road
Penzance,
Cornwall
TR18 4FF
South West
+44 (0)17 3636 9224
jubileepool.co.uk

Penzance's triangular, art deco lido has been welcoming swimmers since it opened in the 1930s. These days the salt water pool is not just a draw in the warmer summer months, thanks to a section of the pool that is naturally heated to a toasty 35 °C. Jubilee Pool, which sticks right out into the sea, is both the largest and the first geothermally heated lido in England, using warmth from underground hot water springs. A good reason to jump right in at the deep end.

146 **THAMES LIDO**

Napier Road
Reading,
Berkshire
RG1 8FR
South East
+44 (0)11 8207 0640
thameslido.com

Tucked away, besides the Thames and just minutes from Reading's busy train station, this little technicolour haven of tranquillity is totally unexpected. The current Thames Lido started welcoming swimmers in 2017, after a sensitive restoration of an abandoned former Ladies Swimming Bath which originally opened in 1902. It's now a stunning space, complete with a hot tub, a sauna, spa treatment rooms and a light-filled pool-side restaurant and bar with Mediterranean holiday vibes for refuelling after a dip. Heaven.

147 BRISTOL LIDO

Oakfield Place
Bristol
BS8 2BJ
South West
+44 (0)11 7933 9530
lidobristol.com

Thames Lido's sister site in Bristol is just as much of a hidden gem, surrounded by pastel painted Clifton townhouses on a quiet residential street. Pre-book a session in the restored (and now heated) swimming pool, or enjoy drinks and a meal with a view of the water in its buzzy glass-fronted bar and restaurant.

148 HATHERSAGE POOL

Oddfellows Road
Hathersage,
Derbyshire
S32 1DU
Central England
+44 (0)14 3365 0843
hathersage
swimmingpool.co.uk

For an unusual dip with a difference, head to Hathersage Pool in the Peak District. The 30-metre-long lido – which is open all year, whatever the weather, thanks to its comfortable 28 °C temperature – hosts monthly night swims, accompanied by live music. Don't fancy doing the butterfly after dark? You can also swim during daylight hours, when you can also appreciate the village's rural vistas.

149 ILKLEY LIDO

Denton Road
Ilkley,
West Yorkshire
LS29 0BZ
North East
+44 (0)19 4343 6201
bradford.gov.uk

You get ace views from this Grade II-listed lido, which dates back to the 1930s. The lagoon-shaped pool is in a dreamy spot at the southern tip of the Yorkshire Dales, surrounded by greenery and historic moorland. Make use of the lawned picnic area on sunny days, or head indoors where you'll find a cafe and an indoor pool too.

150 PELLS POOL

Brook St
Lewes,
East Sussex
BN7 2BA
South East
+44 (0)12 7347 2334
pellspool.org.uk

One for the warmer months of the year, unheated Pells Pool is the oldest documented freshwater outdoor public lido in England. The spring-fed pool celebrated its 160th anniversary in 2021, and continues to welcome thousands of swimmers each summer. Bring your own coffee cup for a discount from the on-site cafe.

151 SALTDEAN LIDO

Park Road
Saltdean,
East Sussex
BN2 8SP
South East
+44 (0)12 7306 9984
saltdeanlido.org

This art deco beauty is Grade II*-listed, which makes it one of the most historically significant lidos in England. The crescent-shaped pool has recently been restored to its former glory and is open for business, while the accompanying 1930s building, which contains a grand ballroom, is currently in the process of being saved. When it's completed it'll feature a cafe, library, exercise studio and community space.

152 CLEVELAND POOLS

Hampton Row
Bath,
Somerset
BA2 6BJ
South West
clevelandpools.org.uk

Chances are you've never heard of Cleveland Pools, despite it being England's oldest outdoor swimming pool. The lido has been out of action since the 1980s – if you don't count a short stint as a trout farm. Thankfully the fish are now long gone, and the restored, riverside site, which was originally built in 1815, started welcoming visitors again in 2022.

HAUNTED *places*

153 PLUCKLEY

Kent
South East
pluckley.net

This pretty village in rural Kent is proud of its label as the most haunted village in England. Pluckley's official website shares information on local schools, road closures, community events... and where you might encounter any one of the village's 12 ghostly residents. Fancy your chances? Hang around until dusk and you might come face to face with The White Lady, The Red Lady and the ghost of a small white dog in the graveyard of St Nicholas' Church. Or hear a phantom coach and horses rattle through the village streets. Try any of Pluckley's pubs if you have no luck – they all have their own stories of otherworldly apparitions.

154 MANNINGTREE

Essex
East of England

The Essex town of Manningtree is where self-professed Witchfinder General Matthew Hopkins lived in the 1600s. He was responsible for the deaths of hundreds of women in East Anglia's witch trials, and some say you can feel the ancient anger of the persecuted here. There have also been reports of the ghost of Hopkins himself. Sightings have allegedly occurred during full moons in the neighbouring village of Mistley, by the pond where he infamously drowned so many innocent people.

155 BLICKLING HALL

Aylsham,
Norfolk
NR11 6NF
East of England
+44 (0)12 6373 8030
nationaltrust.org.uk

According to legend, you could spot the headless ghost of Anne Boleyn, King Henry VIII's famous second wife, here. Some say she returns to this grand Norfolk hall, which was built on the site of her childhood home, every May on the anniversary of her execution. She's not the only spirit who has supposedly been spotted either. Her father has also been seen roaming the nearby countryside, while you might come across two other former homeowners inside the hall, too.

153 PLUCKLEY

HONISTER SLATE MINE

EXPERIENCES ⚡

Breathtaking **HIKES**

156 **THE RIDGEWAY**

STARTS AT:
OVERTON HILL
Avebury,
Wiltshire
SN8 1QG
South West
nationaltrail.co.uk

Often described as England's oldest road, the Ridgeway is an ancient trail linking Avebury in Wiltshire to Ivinghoe Beacon in Buckingham. The path has been used for millennia, historically by travellers, traders, soldiers and animal herders – it's now traversed by hikers and cyclists instead. The remote route follows a ridge of chalk hills for 87 miles (140 kilometres), offering views of the North Wessex Downs and later the Chilterns. You'll pass through ancient forests and past archaeological monuments like the Uffington White Horse and Wayland's Smithy, a neolithic burial chamber. It would take you approximately six days to walk the entire route, but it's easily broken up into smaller walks if you're pressed for time. The Ridgeway might not lead you through the most dramatic scenery, but this understated walking trail has a lot of atmosphere. If you're open to it, you can feel the history underneath your feet with every step.

157 RAVENSCAR TO ROBIN HOOD'S BAY CIRCULAR

STARTS AT:
THE NATIONAL TRUST
COASTAL CENTRE
Ravenscar,
North Yorkshire
YO13 0NE
North East
nationaltrail.co.uk

An 11-mile (18-kilometre) circular walk through some of North York Moor's best bits, this trek takes in rough moorland, craggy sea cliffs, the old Scarborough-to-Whitby railway line and the sand of Robin Hood's Bay – if the tide is out during your walk, that is. The coastal section is a stretch of the Cleveland Way, a national trail which loops through North Yorkshire, with an in-land detour to Howdale Moor to showcase the unique landscapes this pretty county has to offer.

158 THE OLD MAN OF CONISTON

Coniston,
Cumbria
LA21 8HX
North West

Hiking to the summit of Scafell Pike, the highest mountain in England, might seem like the obvious thing to do if you find yourself in the Lake District, but there are joys to be found on quieter, less well-trodden fells too. The Old Man of Coniston is over 800 metres high, the tallest mountain in the Furness Fells, and the hike up, which is moderately challenging, is well worth the views you're rewarded with (on a clear day) at the top. Climb from Coniston village – there are a number of car parks, like Walna Scar car park, just outside the village which are great places to begin your ascent – and you can rest your legs at The Sun pub for a well-deserved pint afterwards.

159 PENNINE WAY

STARTS AT:
MARY'S LANE
Edale,
Derbyshire
S33 7ZD
Central England
nationaltrail.co.uk

Up for a challenge? This is the toughest of England's national trails. The combined ascent exceeds the height of Mount Everest and you can expect to be walking for up to 20 days, if you do the entire way in one go. The Pennine Way runs from Edale in Derbyshire to Kirk Yetholm, which is just over the Scottish border beyond Hadrian's Wall. The hiking route leads you through England's wildest, hard-to-reach landscapes, along ridges and epic valleys, winding through the Peak District, the Yorkshire Dales and the North Pennines before reaching Northumberland and beyond. It makes for a hilly, incredibly remote and seriously picturesque 268 miles (431 kilometres).

160 LYNMOUTH TO COMBE MARTIN

STARTS AT:
THE ESPLANADE
Lynmouth,
Devon
EX35 6EQ
South West
southwestcoast
path.org.uk

This coastal trek takes you from quaint Lynmouth and Lynton, with its scenic clifftop railway, through the stunning Valley of the Rocks, an otherworldly landscape complete with feral goats, up the Great Hangman peak and beyond. It's just under 14 miles (23 kilometres) of the 630-mile (1014-kilometre) South West Coast Path. Challenging yet beautiful, it's doable in a day, though you can easily break it into smaller sections. Or, alternatively, just keep walking – the entire SWCP route runs from Minehead in Somerset to Poole in Dorset, clinging closely to the coastline as it goes through Devon and Cornwall. Got 52 days to spare? This is the way to spend it.

ADRENALINE *adventures*

161 THE WAVE

AT: WASHINGPOOL FARM
Main Road
Easter Compton,
Bristol
BS35 5RE
South West
+44 (0)33 3016 4133
thewave.com

Want to catch some waves? England probably isn't the first place that springs to mind, but The Wave might just change that. In a rural spot near Bristol, The Wave is England's first inland surf destination. It boasts safe and consistently perfect waves – one every 10 seconds – all year round. You can book surfing lessons to learn how to ride gentle 0,5-metre waves or non-guided surf sessions, with waves that vary in difficulty up to 2-metre barrel waves. You can even camp out onsite beside the surfing lake in safari-style tents until you properly master the art.

162 HONISTER SLATE MINE

Honister Pass
Borrowdale,
Cumbria
CA12 5XN
North West
+44 (0)17 6877 7230
honister.com

A working slate mine in the Lake District, Honister is also home to some seriously thrilling adventures. Head here if the Lakes' hikes and high points aren't cutting it for climbing, canyoning and cliff camping (yep, that's a thing). You'll find the longest high wire bridge in Europe and Via Ferrata Xtreme, a tough guided climb where you're secured to the mountain using cables. Top it off with a 30-metre free fall at the end if your nerves can take it.

163 DREAMLAND MARGATE

Marine Terrace
Margate,
Kent
CT9 1XJ
South East
dreamland.co.uk

Discover a slightly gentler way to get your kicks at Margate's vintage amusement park. It's the oldest surviving theme park in England, and dates back to the 1870s. These days, as well as being a venue for parties, festivals and performances, you'll find street food, a retro roller disco and restored vintage rides. Get your heart racing (or at least pumping a little faster) on the dodgems or the chair-o-plane.

164 COASTEERING

WITH: FORE / ADVENTURE
STARTS AT:
THE HUTQUARTERS
Middle Beach
Car Park
Studland,
Dorset
BH19 3AP
South West
+44 (0)19 2976 1515
foreadventure.co.uk

If you've mastered the bracing English sea swim, take your coastal adventure to the next level. Fore / Adventure run coasteering sessions along Dorset's incredible stretch of the Jurassic Coast, where you make your way along the water's edge in a more daring way. You'll be rock-hopping, scrambling, swell-riding and cliff-jumping in no time. They also run foraging sessions where you can learn to spot edible seaweeds and sea vegetables, so you might even get a salty snack at the end of your adventure.

165 CAVING

WITH: LOST EARTH
ADVENTURES
Settle,
North Yorkshire
BD24 0HX
North East
+44 (0)19 0450 0094
*lostearth
adventures.co.uk*

You might want to give this one a miss if tight spaces stress you out. Lost Earth Adventures take groups under the ground for all kinds of caving adventures. This one, which takes in Long Churns and Wilsons Cave beneath the Yorkshire Dales, is suitable for beginners with more challenging sections for seasoned cavers. It's a little reminder that there are passageways to be traversed and waterfalls and pools to be waded through right beneath our feet.

A N I M A L *encounters*

166 **PORT LYMPNE RESERVE**

Aldington Road
Lympne,
Kent
CT21 4PD
South East
*aspinall
foundation.org*

You don't go to Kent expecting to spot a giraffe, but that's exactly what you'll find at Port Lympne Reserve, which describes itself as a 'breeding sanctuary for rare and endangered animals'. More than 75 species call this park home, living in large leafy enclosures, including barbary lions, which have been extinct in the wild since the 1940s.

167 **BLAKENEY POINT**

Morston Quay
Blakeney,
Norfolk
NR25 7BH
East of England
+44 (0)12 6374 0241
nationaltrust.org.uk

Norfolk's Blakeney Point, within Blakeney National Nature Reserve, is home to the largest grey seal colony in England. You can't reach them by foot or by car, only by boat. Trips leave from Morston Quay or nearby Blakeney Quay, and take you through the creek and out into the open sea to spot seals sunbathing on sandbanks and secluded beaches.

168 KNEPP SAFARIS

New Barn Farm
Swallows Lane
Dial Post,
West Sussex
RH13 8NN
South East
+44 (0)14 0371 3230
kneppsafaris.co.uk

Knepp is a 3500-acre estate in Kent, made up of land that was previously intensely farmed. Since 2001 it's been rewilded, and seen huge increases in wildlife. You can get up close to the changed landscape by booking a safari. There are no tigers or elephants to be spotted here; the sights are on a smaller scale but no less impressive. Think rare butterflies, beavers, storks, kingfishers, nightingales, bats, owls, deer and wild horses.

169 BEAR WOOD

AT: WILD PLACE
PROJECT
Blackhorse Hill,
Bristol
BS10 7TP
South West
+44 (0)11 7428 5602
wildplace.org.uk

European brown bears, grey wolves, lynxes and wolverines wander freely in these 7.5 acres of ancient woodland, just like they would have done in England thousands of years ago. You can spot these once native species in the dense greenery without disturbing them from a wooden walkway, which leads you through the treetops.

170 NORTH SEA OBSERVATORY

Chapel St Leonards,
Lincolnshire
PE24 5XQ
Central England
+44 (0)15 2255 2222
lincolnshire.gov.uk

Sat on the edge of the North Sea, beside beach huts and sand dunes, this bold building is the only purpose-built marine observatory in England. From inside, you get stellar views of the waves (with cups of tea and without the bracing sea breeze, if it's a chilly day). Binoculars are provided to gaze along the beach and out to the sea. Depending on the time of year, you might see wild swans, warblers and grebes, or the thousands of swallows and house martins that roost nearby in the reedbeds.

171 BROWNSEA ISLAND

Poole Harbour
Poole,
Dorset
BH13 7EE
South West
+44 (0)12 0270 7744
nationaltrust.org.uk

A woodland-covered island in the middle of Poole Harbour, Brownsea is worth a visit for a bunch of reasons, but animal lovers flock there because of the island's thriving population of red squirrels. Now endangered, red squirrels are actually native to England but their numbers have dwindled dramatically since the introduction of American grey squirrels. The population here is safe thanks to its island location, and the little creatures are best spotted in autumn scurrying around between the trees.

172 NEW FOREST NATIONAL PARK

Hampshire
South East
newforestnpa.gov.uk

Take a walk or a drive through the New Forest and you are guaranteed to spot a wild New Forest pony. There are around 5000 of them wandering freely around the open forest and grazing in the woods and moorland. They are a gentle breed, but they are semi-feral so it's best to give the ponies space, and be sure to drive carefully around the forest as they often step out onto the roads. Ponies aren't the only animals you can spot around the New Forest – keep your eyes peeled for free-roaming cattle, donkeys, deer and, at some times of year, pigs.

173 FARNE ISLANDS

Near Seahouses,
Northumberland
North East
+44 (0)12 8938 9244
nationaltrust.org.uk

Off the rugged coast of Northumberland, the Farne Islands are home to an incredible breeding seabird colony. Twenty-three species of bird frequent the island, including puffins, guillemots, kittiwakes, Arctic terns and eider ducks, among others. Grey seals also call this rocky outcrop home. The islands can only be accessed by boat. Some trips circle the group of islands while others land on Inner Farne and Staple island, when they are open to the public. Visitors that intend to get off and explore the islands should brush their clothes down and rinse their shoes beforehand, and ensure any food is kept in a sealed container, to protect the islands' special ecosystem.

174 WILDER BLEAN

AT: WEST BLEAN AND
THORNDEN WOODS
NATURE RESERVE
Sturry, near
Canterbury,
Kent
CT6 7NZ
South East
+44 (0)16 2266 2012
*kentwildlife
trust.org.uk*

Wild bison have recently been reintroduced to a patch of ancient woodland in Kent, in the hope that they will provide a sustainable solution to woodland management, allowing us humans to step back from managing the woods. What does that mean? Their natural behaviours such as grazing, felling trees, dust bathing and eating bark will allow other species to thrive and restore the natural biodiversity of West Blean Woods. There's currently a herd of four bison, including a surprise bison calf which was born in autumn 2022, roaming the woodland alongside Exmoor ponies and Iron Age pigs. You might be able to spot them from signposted walks through the woodland.

RAILWAY *routes*

175 BLUEBELL RAILWAY

Sheffield Park
Station
Sheffield Park,
East Sussex
TN22 3QL
South East
+44 (0)18 2572 0800
bluebell-railway.com

Previously part of a working train line between Lewes and East Grinstead, which was closed in the late 1950s, Bluebell Railway is now 11 miles (18 kilometres) of perfectly preserved railway. Vintage steam trains and carriages now carry visitors along the track, which runs from Sheffield Park to East Grinstead, with stations along the way at Horsted Keynes and Kingscote. Each of the Bluebell Line's stations are charmingly frozen in time, showcasing different periods of the railway's history.

176 GREAT CENTRAL RAILWAY

Loughborough
Central Station
Great Central Road
Loughborough,
Leicestershire
LE11 1RW
Central England
+44 (0)15 0963 2323
gcrailway.co.uk

One for dedicated train fans, Great Central Railway is the only double track heritage railway in the country, meaning it's the only place where full size steam engines can be seen passing each other at speed on the rails. Vintage steam locomotives and diesel railcars run along the route, which can take visitors to Leicester and back. Visit when there's a special event on, like fish and chip suppers or a vintage vehicle rally, to really see the railway come alive.

177 THE WATERCRESS LINE

The Railway Station
Alresford,
Hampshire
SO24 9JG
South East
+44 (0)19 6273 3810
watercressline.co.uk

Opened in 1865, the Mid-Hants Railway was built to connect existing train lines, creating an alternative route from London to Southampton – and to help transport the peppery watercress grown in the beds around Alresford to be sold, hence the current name. The line closed in the 1970s, and now only the section of track between Alton and Alresford remains in use as a heritage railway, populated with gleaming steam trains. Each of the line's stations is a glorious time capsule, even more so on special days when staff and visitors are encouraged to come in vintage dress. The line also runs a number of themed events, like festive Steam Illuminations and boozy Real Ale Train evenings.

178 RIVIERA LINE

Exeter St Davids
Train Station
Bonhay Road
Exeter,
Devon
EX4 4NT
South West

You'll just need a regular train ticket to ride the Riviera Line, a name for the stretch of railway that runs between Exeter and Paignton. Here the line hugs closely to the sea wall, meaning you have land to your right and the waves to your left. After leaving the city of Exeter, you pass beside the Exe Estuary, whizzing through pretty seaside towns like Dawlish and Teignmouth, where the line dips inland for a while before rejoining the coast at Torquay and finally reaching Paignton. On rough weather days waves have been known to breach the rails, and even destroyed part of the line during a severe storm in 2014, but it's usually a calm ride with mega sea views.

CANALWAYS *to explore*

179 **STANDEDGE TUNNEL**

Waters Road
Marsden,
West Yorkshire
HD7 6NQ
North East
+44 (0)14 8424 2792
canalrivertrust.org.uk

Standedge Tunnel is the longest, deepest and highest canal tunnel in England. There are actually four tunnels that disappear into the Pennine Hills – three of them are railway tunnels and one is a waterway that you can ride through on a canal boat. Glide under the hills through the atmospheric tunnel on a boat trip, or even steer your own vessel through the gloom.

180 **BRADFORD-ON-AVON**

Wiltshire
BA15 1LE
South West

Charming Bradford-on-Avon is populated with ancient buildings and buzzy cafes and shops, all centred around the water. Both the River Avon and the Kennet and Avon Canal flow through and around the town. A walk alongside the canal, behind the town's ancient Tithe Barn, will reveal colourful barges and floating shops, while from the town's wharf you can easily hop on board a boat to explore the area's lush countryside. The *Barbara McLellan* is a green and red boat that runs regular public trips along the local canalways. You can also book her out for private jaunts along the water.

181 FOXTON LOCKS

Foxton,
Leicestershire
LE16 7RA
Central England
+44 (0)11 6279 3686
canalrivertrust.org.uk

On a rural stretch of the Leicester section of the Grand Union Canal you'll find a series of stepped canal locks that is actually the longest and steepest staircase flight of locks in England. Foxton Locks is made up of ten locks that help passing canal boats climb or descend a steep hill. You can ride the staircase if you've chartered your own boat, or, if that all seems like quite a lot of hard work, you can simply watch the boats make their journeys up and down. Luckily there are pubs and cafes at either end.

Historic **S P A S**

182 **SPA VILLAGE BATH**

AT: THE GAINSBOROUGH
BATH SPA
Beau St
Bath,
Somerset
BA1 1QY
South West
+44 (0)12 2535 8888
*thegainsborough
bathspa.co.uk*

It's no secret that Bath is a historic spa city.
The Roman baths in the city centre are a popular
tourist attraction, while the Thermae Bath Spa is
famous for allowing visitors to wallow in the city's
naturally warm waters just as the Romans once
did. But if you want to share your spa experience
with fewer people, you might want to consider
a trip to Spa Village Bath. Opened in 2015, the
Gainsborough hotel's basement spa is unique
in that it taps into Bath's mineral-rich, ancient
thermal springs. Hotel and spa guests can take the
waters through a self-guided circuit of two thermal
pools, a steam room, two saunas and an ice alcove.
Fancy even more privacy while you bathe? Bath
Spa rooms in the hotel feature bathrooms that tap
into the famous waters too.

183 TURKISH BATHS HARROGATE

183 TURKISH BATHS HARROGATE

Parliament St
Harrogate,
North Yorkshire
HG1 2WH
North East
+44 (0)14 2355 6746
*turkishbaths
harrogate.co.uk*

Harrogate's natural spring waters were discovered in 1571 but it was the Victorians who built this beautiful temple to wellness in the town. Very few alterations have been made over the years and the baths, with their Moorish design, terrazzo floors and intricate arches and painted ceilings, are now the most historically complete Turkish bath left in England. Visitors can still move between the frigidarium, the steam room, three heated chambers and a cold plunge pool. A relaxing spa treatment menu, featuring a dreamy Turkish spa body ritual, is a welcome modern addition.

184 BUXTON CRESCENT HEALTH SPA HOTEL

The Crescent
Buxton,
Derbyshire
SK17 6BH
Central England
+44 (0)12 9880 8999
ensanahotels.com

Buxton's thermal spring made the town, at one point, a leading spa destination that rivalled Bath. That's when Buxton Crescent, which is similar in style to Bath's Royal Crescent, was built. After years of neglect, the 18th-century crescent has recently been restored to its former glory and is now home to a luxury hotel as well as an extensive spa that utilises the town's ancient thermal spring.

THOR'S CAVE

LANDSCAPES ⏚

Secluded **BEACHES**

185 **THE STRANGLES**

Crackington Haven,
Cornwall
EX23 0LQ
South West

This beach takes quite some effort to get to (and back out of) but the exertion is well worth it. The Strangles is signposted from the coastal road and the South West Coast Path, a little south of Crackington Haven. To begin with, the path takes you past hedgerows and fields before it opens out to expansive views of the Atlantic. Here the route becomes steep and sometimes slippery underfoot, as you start to meander down the cliff, past heather and gorse flowers, to the beach below. When you've made it you'll most likely be rewarded with a stretch of magical coastline, complete with a rock arch, all to yourself. At worst you'll share it with a couple of other intrepid beach-goers. Unsurprisingly there are no facilities at The Strangles, so you'd be wise to pack a picnic to fuel your ascent back up the path.

186 **FORMBY BEACH**

Formby,
Merseyside
L37 1LJ
North West
+44 (0)17 0487 8591
nationaltrust.org.uk

Okay, so on a sunny day, when visitors flock here in their droves, Formby can hardly be called a hidden gem. But visit out of season and you'll be surprised to find this great swathe of pristine sand dune and sea, so close to a major city like Liverpool. Visit to discover silent forests, red squirrels, incredible dunes, miles of soft sand and the outlines of shipwrecks just off the coast.

187 HOLKHAM BEACH

AT: HOLKHAM NATIONAL
NATURE RESERVE
Lady Anne's Drive
Norfolk
NR23 1RG
East of England
+44 (0)13 2871 3111
holkham.co.uk

Holkham Beach isn't exactly an under-the-radar beach – it often graces 'best of' lists. But it's such a spacious and impressive stretch of coastline that you can always find a corner of sand to call your own and each visit feels like a brand-new discovery. Backed by a nature reserve and peaceful pine forest, visitors must pad quietly through the trees before reaching dunes and then sand that, at low tide, feels like it stretches away for miles before meeting the sea.

188 RUMBLING KERN

Howick,
Northumberland
NE66 3LH
North East

If it feels like there's something secretive about this tiny beach, it won't come as a surprise to learn that it was apparently once used by smugglers. The petite patch of sand is sheltered by small cliffs and unaffected by high tides, making it a perfect picnic spot. The beach is named for a rock formation on the other side of the cliffs. Climb up and over to see a huge cavity carved in the rock by the sea, which makes a loud rumbling noise as the waves pass through.

189 HAYBURN WYKE

Crowdon,
North Yorkshire
YO12 6LD
North East

You'll find pebbles, rocks, even boulders at Hayburn Wyke but no sand. This is a beach for dramatics rather than sunbathing. Trees and shrubbery tumble down to the coastline here, where they meet the North Sea. It's all arresting, but the best spot of all is the Hayburn Wyke waterfall, which falls down into a huge rockpool on the beach. Bring a flask of tea and perch on one of the boulders besides the water for a while to really take it all in.

190 WORBARROW BAY

Tyneham,
Dorset
BH20 5QF
South West
visit-dorset.com

Worbarrow Bay can be a little tricky to get to, but that means you can often have the entire sweep of the Jurassic Coast cove to yourself. The sheltered spot, which is great for a peaceful sea swim, is reached via the South West Coast Path or by a short walk from Tyneham village (another place that was evacuated in 1943 to be used for military training and never returned to the villagers) – but both Tyneham and Worbarrow are managed by the Ministry of Defence, so access is only allowed when the Lulworth Army Ranges are not in use. Check before you visit, and stick strictly to the paths when you do. Nearby Chapman's Pool is another beach only accessible when the MoD allow – it's a peaceful cove a similar shape to much busier Lulworth Cove, which is just west along the coast.

191 PEPPERCOMBE BEACH

Peppercombe,
Devon
EX39 5EA
South West

A wide, pebbly stretch of coastline where you might not see another soul, Peppercombe Beach is at the bottom of a deep wooded valley. It's the ultimate unspoilt beach, backed by red sandstone cliffs and without a penny arcade in sight. Or a car park, for that matter. Access is by foot only and there's no nearby parking, so many visitors leave their cars at nearby Bucks Mills and walk the South West Coast Path over to Peppercombe. On the path down to the beach you will find The Coach House, a little shelter maintained by the National Trust that might come in handy as an emergency picnic spot if the English weather isn't kind.

Secret **GARDENS**

192 **THE LOST GARDENS OF HELIGAN**

Pentewan,
Cornwall
PL26 6EN
South West
+44 (0)17 2684 5100
heligan.com

Once magnificent, these gardens were almost lost forever when the Heligan estate was abandoned during WWI. The gardeners who had tended to the acres went to war and weeds and brambles took over. The gardens were rediscovered and renovations began to return them to their former glory in 1990. Now the romantic gardens are full of intrigue and surprise, and feature blousy blooms, kitchen gardens, glasshouses growing exotic fruit, a subtropical jungle and meadows. Head to Heligan's woodland to stumble upon a series of surreal sculptures, like *Mudmaid*, a moss-covered figure asleep on the forest floor who changes with the seasons.

193 THE WALLED GARDEN

AT: MOTTISFONT

Mottisfont Lane
Near Romsey,
Hampshire
SO51 0LP
South East
+44 (0)17 9434 0757
nationaltrust.org.uk

When the roses are out at Mottisfont, the heady scent of petals hits you before you even step foot inside the Walled Garden. From there, the gardens are a sensory delight, best visited in June when gravel pathways lead you through two walled gardens, past petite lawns, water features and benches surrounded by a riotous display of mid-summer flowers. There's more to see than roses, but they are the stars of the show, climbing over stone walls, clambering up arches and blooming in countless pastel shades.

194 TRESCO ABBEY GARDEN

Tresco, Isles of Scilly,
Cornwall
TR24 0QQ
South West
+44 (0)17 2042 2849
tresco.co.uk

The Scilly Isles are an unspoilt archipelago just off the English coast that, thanks to their white sandy beaches and bobbing palm trees, can feel a lot further away in the summer months. Planted in the 19th century around the ruins of an ancient abbey, Tresco Abbey Garden is an especially otherworldly corner of Tresco Island, packed with more than 4000 plant specimens from the southern hemisphere that thrive in the island's subtropical climate.

195 LEVENS HALL GARDENS

Kendal,
Cumbria
LA8 0PD
North West
+44 (0)15 3956 0321
levenshall.co.uk

Foliage archways and bold shapes sculpted out of ancient box and yew await at Levens Hall Gardens, the oldest topiary gardens in the world which date back to the 1690s. These 10 acres of gardens remain largely unchanged by the centuries. As well as an impressive topiary collection, visitors will find orchards, beautiful borders, rose gardens, lawns and meadows.

196 SISSINGHURST CASTLE GARDEN

Biddenden Road
Sissinghurst,
Kent
TN17 2AB
South East
+44 (0)15 8071 0700
nationaltrust.org.uk

If you feel like there's something poetic about the gardens at Sissinghurst, you won't be surprised to learn that they are quite literally the stuff of poetry. They were designed and planted by author and poet Vita Sackville-West, who moved here with her husband politician and writer Harold Nicolson in the 1930s. The garden is diverse and intriguing; each space has its own theme. The Cottage Garden blooms in shades of reds and golds, The Purple Border is a heady mix of blues, pinks and lilacs, while The White Garden erupts in pale gladioli, dahlias and anemones. For fragrance as well as beauty visit The Herb Garden.

197 PAINSWICK ROCOCO GARDEN

Painswick,
Gloucestershire
GL6 6TH
South West
+44 (0)14 5281 3204
rococogarden.org.uk

This playful, ornamental garden is tucked away in the middle of the Cotswolds' simple rolling hills. It's England's only complete surviving rococo garden, designed in the 1740s as a flamboyant pleasure garden for entertaining guests. The original design was lost to nature over the years, but has been painstakingly restored in the last half century. Now, visitors can discover follies and perfectly framed views within a hidden valley. Visit in very early spring to see Painswick transformed by a frost-like carpet of snowdrops.

Deserted **FORESTS**

198 **GRIZEDALE FOREST**

Hawkshead,
Cumbria
LA22 0QJ
North West
+44 (0)30 0067 4495
forestryengland.uk

The Lake District is known for its glassy bodies of water, but the National Park also does good woodland. Grizedale Forest is 8000 acres of stunning ancient forest, scored with pretty walking, cycling and horse-riding trails (as well as zip wires through the trees if you're feeling adventurous). It's a peaceful place to visit at any time of year, but especially so in autumn when you can catch the leaves turning vibrant shades of rust and gold.

199 **WISTMAN'S WOOD**

AT: DARTMOOR
NATIONAL PARK
Two Bridges,
Devon
South West

This remote patch of woodland might be small, but its atmosphere is mighty. You'll discover gnarled oak trees that, high up in the heart of Dartmoor where the weather changes suddenly and dramatically, have stood strong against the elements for centuries. Big boulders and exposed tree roots, all covered in soft green moss and lichen, run across the forest floor ready to trip you up. It's an incredible place that's said to have inspired myth and legend over the years – some say the woodland is haunted, home to pixies and even visited by hellhounds.

200 PUZZLEWOOD

Perrygrove Road
Coleford,
Gloucestershire
GL16 8QB
South West
+44 (0)15 9483 3187
puzzlewood.net

Dense, mossy greenery and strange rock formations make up these 14 acres of ancient woodland in the Forest of Dean. Paths and wooden bridges lead walkers through the ethereal and enchanting forest. No surprise that it's said to have been an inspiration for *The Lord of the Rings* author J.R.R. Tolkien and for the forbidden forest in the *Harry Potter* books. The forest has also welcomed stormtroopers, time lords, giants and wizards as an atmospheric filming location – but despite its popularity you can still find a stretch of silent woodland to enjoy without another soul in sight.

201 BOLDERWOOD

Ornamental Drive
Near Lyndhurst,
Hampshire
SO43 7GE
South East
+44 (0)30 0067 4601
forestryengland.uk

Despite its name, the New Forest isn't, as you might expect, all forest. The area is made up of moors, heathland, coastline and woodland, all dotted with villages (and the area's wild ponies, of course). To find yourself surrounded by peaceful, ancient trees, head to Bolderwood. Here you can discover a mix of grand old trees dating back to 1860 and ornamental woodland, as well as a viewing area for spotting wild herds of deer. There are a number of marked walking routes in the area, as well as ace places to stop for a picnic beneath the branches.

Atmospheric **ISLANDS**

202 **MERSEA ISLAND**

Essex

East of England

visitmersea

island.co.uk

Just under 7000 people call Mersea Island home. There's plenty of space for visitors to explore the unique coastal spot, known for its colourful beach huts and super-fresh seafood. East Mersea is the place to head if you fancy walking in nature and exploring rural beaches, while West Mersea is where you'll find a busier beach backed by a small fishing town. This is where you want to be if a plate of Colchester oysters and a glass of Mersea Island Vineyard white appeals. The only way on and off the island is via The Strood causeway, which sometimes floods at high tide, so plan your travel around low tide times.

203 ST MICHAEL'S MOUNT

Marazion,
Cornwall
TR17 0HS
South West
+44 (0)17 3688 7822
stmichaelsmount.co.uk

There's no claiming St Michael's Mount is off the beaten track. The tidal island near Cornwall's Penzance is one of the most photographed landmarks in England. However, its unique location, at the other side of a causeway accessible only during low tide, makes it by its very nature hidden away from 'real life', especially if you visit outside of Cornwall's busy tourist season. You can walk over to the island a handful of hours a day. Once there, watching the waves lap higher and higher over the stones until your path back to the mainland entirely disappears is a wonderfully strange experience. A tour of the island reveals hidden surprises too, such as the castle's intricate, terraced gardens, studded with succulents, that step down towards the waves.

203 ST MICHAEL'S MOUNT

204 HOLY ISLAND OF LINDISFARNE

Northumberland
TD15 2SE
North East
lindisfarne.org.uk

An otherworldly island in a remote part of Northumberland, Lindisfarne has a big history. It is a spiritual place of pilgrimage, the home of saints and the centre of Christianity in Anglo Saxon times, ransacked by Vikings in the 8th century. Like St Michael's Mount, it's a tidal island, cut off from mainland England at high tide. But, if you can make it across the causeway, there's a little more life to be found on the other side, where there is a small but permanent population. As well as a castle clinging to the coastline and an ancient priory, you'll find cafes, a coffee roasters, pubs, a gin distillery and even places to stay the night on the surreal little island.

205 PIEL ISLAND

Islands of Furness
Cumbria
LA13 0QN
North West
+44 (0)73 8700 8931
pielisland.co.uk

This truly tiny island, sat just off the Furness Peninsula south of the Lake District, is just 50 acres in size. Take the ferry over from Roa Island and you'll find a campsite, a pub and a castle. The ruins of Piel Castle, a 14th-century fortress designed to protect the area from pirates and raiders, are free to explore. The Ship Inn is the heart of the island – uniquely each new pub landlord is crowned 'king' of the island in a strange ceremony which dates back hundreds of years. Enjoying the Piel vibe? Stay the night – the campsite is first-come-first-served and just around £5 per tent.

206 ST MARY'S

Isles of Scilly
Cornwall
South West
visitislesofscilly.com

Each of the Scilly islands are atmospheric in their own way. There are hundreds of them – only five inhabited – sitting just off the coast of Cornwall and accessed via ferry, helicopter or small plane. St Agnes, the most south-westerly, is wild and peaceful, Bryher tiny and rugged, St Martin's is known for its stunning beaches while privately-owned Tresco is the fanciest of the bunch. St Mary's is the biggest of the Scillies, the gateway to the rest of the islands, and it's dotted with hidden treasures. As well as lush beaches and dramatic coastline, you can find a number of well-preserved prehistoric sites that offer a glimpse into the islands' incredible history. Don't miss Porth Hellick Down, a burial chamber whose style is unique to these islands and mainland Cornwall, or Halangy Down, the remains of an ancient Iron Age village.

H I L L S *and high places*

207 MALHAM COVE

Malham,
North Yorkshire
BD23 4DG
North East

Malham Cove isn't exactly a secret – you might even recognise it from scenes in the *Harry Potter* films – but it's in this book because seeing the majestic limestone cliffs rise up as you approach alongside Malham Beck is never not surprising. The gently curved cliff face, miles from the coast in the Yorkshire Dales, is around 70 metres high. A footpath from Malham village will lead you to the foot of the cliff and you'll find steps that take you to the summit, where you'll find an unusual limestone pavement (a naturally occurring rock formation that looks like paving slabs) with mega views.

207 MALHAM COVE

208 PENDLE HILL

**Barley Lane
Barley,
Lancashire
BB9 6LG
North West**

At 557 metres above sea level, Pendle Hill is a significant landmark, which gives its name to the local area. A fairly steep step-like path leads you up to the top, and from the summit you get unbeatable views of the Ribble Valley and the Lancashire and Yorkshire countryside. Pendle Hill has an interesting history too. It's known for the Pendle Witch Trials in 1612 (which are among the most famous witch trials to take place in England) where twelve people living in the Pendle Hill area were charged with witchcraft. Ten were found guilty and sentenced to death. The memory of the trials lives on, with ghost walks taking place most Halloweens.

209 UPPARK HOUSE

**South Harting,
West Sussex
GU31 5QR
South East
+44 (0)17 3082 5415
*nationaltrust.org.uk***

On a clear day you can see the south coast from the grounds of Uppark, a grand 17th-century house set high up on a hill in the South Downs, close to the South Downs Way walking trail. Despite being miles inland, its spot on the South Downs ridge affords it mega views – it also means the manor house is rather exposed to the weather so can be especially chilly and windy in the winter months. Luckily there's a cafe and secondhand bookshop on site for hiding away in if needs be.

210 YES TOR

AT: DARTMOOR
NATIONAL PARK
Near Okehampton,
Devon
EX20 4LU
South West

The second highest peak in Dartmoor (nearby High Willhays takes the top spot by a fraction), Yes Tor is 619 metres above sea level. After a craggy climb you are rewarded with incredible vistas, providing Dartmoor's infamous mist hasn't descended – look out for the English Channel to the south and the Atlantic Ocean to your west, as well as glimpses of Exmoor and Bodmin moors. You can approach the tor from all angles, but the easiest way is probably to park at nearby Meldon Reservoir and hike south.

211 ST CATHERINE'S ORATORY

Blackgang Road
Ventnor,
Isle of Wight
PO38 2JB
South East
+44 (0)37 0333 1181
english-heritage.org.uk

St Catherine's Oratory, or the Pepperpot as it is affectionately known, boasts amazing views of the Isle of Wight. The building is positioned on one of the island's highest points and from here you can see the coastline as it curves away to the east and west. There's a good reason this simple structure has such ace sea views – it is England's only surviving medieval lighthouse, built in 1328 by a local landowner as penance for stealing casks of wine from a shipwreck.

212 GOLDEN CAP

Morcombelake,
Dorset
DT6 6SF
South West
+44 (0)12 9748 9481
nationaltrust.org.uk

The highest point on England's south coast, Golden Cap rises out of the Jurassic coastline at 191 metres above sea level, proffering views across Lyme Bay as far as Dartmoor to the west. There are miles of walking routes on the Golden Cap estate to explore. Start at either Stonebarrow Hill or Langdon Hill car parks and take your pick of trails through woodland and grassland to those dreamy sea views.

213 HIGH CUP NICK

Pennine Way
Near Dufton,
Cumbria
CA16 6NF
North West

The rugged North Pennines are home to some of England's most remote and isolated locations. An epic valley, High Cup Nick or High Cup Gill as it is also known, is one of them. The deep valley was carved in the landscape by a glacier thousands and thousands of years ago and is now perfectly u-shaped. High Cup Nick specifically refers to the high point from which you get an incredible view of the sweeping scar. It's on the Pennine Way but you can walk out to the viewpoint from the village of Dufton, either as a there-and-back or a circular, by dropping down into the valley itself. The Nick is around a 4-mile (6,5-kilometre) trek from Dufton's public car park.

214 BRIMHAM ROCKS

Brimham Moor
Road
Summerbridge,
North Yorkshire
HG3 4DW
North East
+44 (0)14 2378 0688
nationaltrust.org.uk

Far from your average moorland, Brimham Moor is covered in weird and wonderful rock formations. The result is otherworldly: half oversized art installation, half reminiscent of an episode of the *Flintstones*. The surreal shapes, stacks and balances have been sculpted by wind and water erosion over millions of years, though there is something atmospheric and almost magical about the rocks, which led to theories in the 18th and 19th centuries that the shapes were carved by druids. If you can tear yourself away from the boulders themselves, check out the views too. From here you can soak up sweeping vistas of the surrounding countryside.

215 KINDER SCOUT

High Peak,
Derbyshire
S33 7ZJ
Central England

The highest point in Derbyshire, Kinder Scout might just be the best viewpoint in the Peak District. A grand moorland plateau at 2087 feet (636 metres) above sea level, from here you can take in the best of the Peaks. On a clear day you can catch a glimpse of Manchester too, or even Wales' Snowdonia National Park in the far distance. There are lots of routes up to pick from, and most start in either Edale or Hayfield. Kinder Scout can get busy on weekends, but there's always space to be found in this huge, wild landscape.

Amazing COASTLINE

216 BOTANY BAY

Marine Drive
Broadstairs,
Kent
CT10 3LG
South East

You'll find Botany Bay's bold chalk stacks on the curve of coastline between Broadstairs and Margate. It's a drop down to the sand from the high cliffs, where residential streets enjoy ace views of the sea. It's a great beach for a day out, with soft sand and rock pools to explore, but the huge natural chalk towers, vibrantly green with seaweed at the bottom and pure white further up, are the real draw.

217 SONG OF THE SEA CAVE

Nanjizal Beach,
Cornwall
TR19 7AH
South West

This secluded beach on Cornwall's Penwith Peninsula really is a hidden gem. Any route to the beach involves a walk and some steep steps down to the sand – start at either Land's End or Porthgwarra Beach and walk along the South West Coast Path until you hit Nanjizal Beach. When you've made it, you'll find a sea cave complete with two natural pools and a narrow rock arch called Song of the Sea. The arch, also known as Zawn Pyg, is especially stunning as the sun starts to go down when golden light illuminates the gap. Aim to visit at low tide on a calm day.

218 BLACKCHURCH ROCK

Mouthmill Beach, Devon
EX39 6AN
South West

From certain angles, Blackchurch Rock looks like a neat art sculpture placed on the beach. The angular double arch stack – a triangle with two windows – is on Mouthmill Beach near Clovelly, on an isolated stretch of coastline. The natural arch sits in the sea at high tide, while you can get a closer look and see the incredible formation from all sides when the tide is out. You can access Mouthmill by walking along the South West Coast Path, or parking at Brownsham National Trust Car Park and making your way down to the beach through woodland.

219 STAIR HOLE

West Lulworth, Dorset
BH20 5RH
South West

The entire Jurassic Coast is known for its incredible rock formations and stunning fossil-studded beaches. Stair Hole is one overlooked and easily missed example, sandwiched between popular Lulworth Cove and rock formation A-lister Durdle Door. It's a pretty little cove boasting caves, arches and a blow hole, all of which have been naturally formed by coastal erosion over the centuries. The clear layers and folds in the rock to the left of Stair Hole, known as the Lulworth Crumple, are a lesson in geology. Take it all in at the viewpoint above the waves.

220 THE DRINKING DINOSAUR

Flamborough Head,
East Riding of Yorkshire
YO15 1AR
North East

A beautiful example of Yorkshire's diverse coastline, you'll find rock stacks, steep cliffs, sea caves and rock arches at Flamborough Head. One of the best is dubbed The Drinking Dinosaur, a rock formation and natural rock arch carved out of the white cliffs that from some angles resembles – you guessed it – a dinosaur drinking from the sea. The area is also a haven for wildlife – you might spot seals or even puffins here.

Gorges and **CAVES**

221 LYDFORD GORGE

Lydford,
Devon
EX20 4BH
South West
+44 (0)18 2282 0320
nationaltrust.org.uk

On the edge of Dartmoor National Park, the River Lyd has cut a deep gorge into the rock, and it now makes a pretty and atmospheric place to explore. You begin your walk up high before making your way down through a steep wooded valley, past little waterfalls, ancient trees, ferns and flora. Then the path leads you past the impressive White Lady waterfall, a 30-metre cascade of water into the Lyd, before taking you alongside the water on smooth, polished rocks. You'll end up at Devil's Cauldron, a roaringly loud pothole at the gorge's deepest part.

222 THOR'S CAVE

Leek Road
Wetton,
Staffordshire
DE6 2AF
Central England

Visible from the ground below, this natural cavern is high up in a limestone hill. It's stunning to spot as you approach, but the best views come when you are inside the cave itself and its opening frames your Peak District surroundings. Take a minute to soak up the inside of the cave itself, which is thought to have provided shelter to people (as well as animals like brown bears) during the Stone Age. There's a small roadside car park from where you can begin your walk up to the cave. Alternatively, you can extend your route by starting in Wetton, or wandering along part of the Manifold Way too.

223 PEAK CAVERN

Peak Cavern Road
Castleton,
Derbyshire
S33 8WS
Central England
+44 (0)14 3362 0285
peakcavern.co.uk

More often known by its other name 'The Devil's Arse', Peak Cavern boasts the largest cave entrance in England. Inside, caverns lead on from one another, each revealing new surprises. The Peak Cavern cave system is extensive, featuring 13 miles (20,5 kilometres) of caves, passageways and shafts, waterfalls and glassy pools. Regular guided tours of the entrance and the Peak Cavern Show Cave are available. Alternatively, book a ticket to a concert put on within the cave entrance to check out its magical acoustics.

224 CRESWELL CRAGS

Crags Road
Creswell,
Nottinghamshire
S80 3LH
Central England
+44 (0)19 0972 0378
creswell-crags.org.uk

A limestone gorge, which itself is free to explore, is home to Creswell's caves, all of which offer a glimpse into prehistoric life in England. You can book tours that take you inside some of the caves, which were home for people during the Ice Age, tens of thousands of years ago. In fact, evidence of human life as well as bears, spotted hyenas, reindeers, lions and woolly mammoths and rhinoceroses have been found here. Check out ancient engravings and witch marks on the walls and learn about the history of the atmospheric space.

225 GORDALE SCAR

Malham,
North Yorkshire
BD23 4DL
North East
+44 (0)30 0456 0030
yorkshiredales.org.uk

A hidden gorge, formed over thousands of years during the Ice Age, the sheer scale of Gordale Scar isn't apparent until you step right into it. The deep ravine is dotted with waterfalls and interesting rock formations – there's a footpath right through the gorge and it's free to explore at any time. Discovering it for yourself feels like a real wow moment.

Wonderful **WATERFALLS**

---

226 ROUGHTING LINN

Broomridgedean
Burn
Northumberland
TD15 2QF
North East

This fairytale-esque waterfall is hidden in a lush wooded valley. To find it you can walk down to Broomridgedean Burn on a narrow path from the nearest road, or take a picturesque route cross country from the nearby village of Ford. When you reach it, you'll find moss-covered stones and overhanging trees framing the waterfall. Wear wellies and wade into the stream for a closer look.

226 ROUGHTING LINN

227 BRONTË WATERFALL

Haworth Moor,
West Yorkshire
BD22 8DR
North East

A gentle waterfall in a picturesque spot, Brontë Waterfall on rugged Haworth Moor is so called because of the area's connection with the Brontë sisters, writers Charlotte, Anne and Emily who between them penned famous works like *Wuthering Heights, Jane Eyre* and *The Tenant of Wildfell Hall*. It's said the sisters sometimes visited the waterfall, while a nearby ruined farmhouse called Top Withens is often credited with inspiring the location of the house Wuthering Heights. You can find both on the Brontë Way walking route. Though not exactly hidden (swarms of literature fans visit each year) nearby Haworth, where the family lived, and its Brontë Parsonage Museum are well worth a visit if you're in the area.

228 LUMB HOLE FALLS

Sunny Bank Road
Hebden Bridge,
West Yorkshire
HX7 8RG
North East

Multiple streams tumble into a pool at Lumb Hole Falls, a lush spot surrounded by trees and mossy rocks. To soak up the stunning Yorkshire scenery, make a walk of it, either setting off from nearby Hebden Bridge or Hardcastle Crags, where there is a National Trust-run car park, to make your way through hilly farmland and forest to reach the waterfall.

229 STOCK GHYLL FORCE

Stockghyll Lane
Ambleside,
Cumbria
LA22 0QT
North West

Just a short walk out of the centre of Ambleside and you'll find yourself face to face with this 70-foot (20-metre) stunner. Though you'll only come across this waterfall if you're looking for it, it was once a very popular attraction – you can find an old revolving gate used by Victorian tourists along the path. Follow signs through the woodland which will lead you past a number of smaller falls before you reach viewing platforms for the main attraction. Once the water has crashed past the trees here, it then streams through the town before joining the River Rothay and flowing into Lake Windermere.

230 SPEKE'S MILL MOUTH WATERFALL

Hartland Quay,
Devon
EX39 6EA
South West

There are a number of coastal waterfalls in this remote and romantic corner of North Devon, which is populated with high rocky cliffs. One brilliant example is Speke's Mill Mouth, which plunges dramatically over the edge of the land and down sheer rock to the beach and sea below. Park at Hartland Quay and walk south along the South West Coast Path to find the magnificent fall. You'll also pass by high point St Catherine's Tor.

MAN-MADE *landscapes*

231 SILBURY HILL

West Kennett,
Wiltshire
SN8 1QH
South West
+44 (0)37 0333 1181
english-heritage.org.uk

You could very easily drive right past this large mound beside the A4. But Silbury Hill is not just, as you might assume, a strange-shaped hill – it's the largest artificial mound in Europe. It was likely completed around 2400 BC and is comparable in size and shape to Egypt's pyramids. Close to the incredible neolithic monuments in and around Avebury, the intriguing hill is thought to hold some significance, but, despite at least three tunnels being dug to its centre in search of answers, we are yet to discover why it was built or what its purpose was to the people who built it. You can pause to view it (visitors are no longer allowed to climb the hill) for free at any time – there's a small car park and viewing area beside the road.

232 CERNE GIANT

Cerne Abbas,
Dorset
DT2 7AL
South West
+44 (0)12 9748 9481
nationaltrust.org.uk

The steep slope above the village of Cerne Abbas in Dorset is adorned with a rather unusual artwork: an 180-foot (55-metre) naked man sculpted into the chalk hillside. It's the largest chalk hill figure (yes, there are others) in England, and the most detailed too. The explicit figure has been hanging out on the hill since the late Saxon period and may have been a symbol of fertility. Birds get the best view, but you can get a good look from the viewing area in Giant's View car park.

233 NORTHUMBER-LANDIA

Blagdon Lane
Cramlington,
Northumberland
NE23 8AU
North East
+44 (0)16 7073 8701
*northumber
landia.com*

It wasn't just ancient peoples who manipulated the land into human-like figures. Completed in 2012, *Northumberlandia* is a huge earthen sculpture of a woman laying down. She's 100 feet (30 metres) high and a quarter of a mile (400 metres) long, made out of 1,5 million tonnes of rock, soil and clay. The figure is covered in grasses, and constantly changing with the seasons. There are four miles (6,5 kilometres) of walking routes on and around her, so take your pick to explore the landscape.

234 UFFINGTON WHITE HORSE

Uffington,
Oxfordshire
SN7 7UK
South East
+44 (017 9376 2209
nationaltrust.org.uk

Here's another figure cut into the chalk, this time of a horse. Carved into the hillside just a little way off The Ridgeway, the horse has been visible since some time between the late Bronze and Iron Ages (dating it precisely has proven a little tricky). It measures 111 metres from tail to ear. You can spy it for miles around, or get up close to it with a walk on White Horse Hill itself.

235 OFFA'S DYKE

Lydney,
Gloucestershire
GL15 6XD
South West
+44 (0)37 0333 1181
english-heritage.org.uk

Did you know that there's an enormous earthwork – a high bank and ditch scored into the ground – that roughly marks the border between England and Wales? It was built under orders of Offa, King of Mercia, sometime around 780 AD. The address listed here is just for a small, but attractive, section of Offa's Dyke which is managed by English Heritage. The dyke runs for over 80 of the 149 miles (130 of the 240 kilometres) between Sedbury in the south and Prestatyn in the north.

DAUNT BOOKS

SHOPPING 🛍

Brilliant **BOOKSHOPS**

236 **BOOK-CYCLE**

7 West St
Exeter,
Devon
EX1 1BB
South West
+44 (0)13 9242 0021
book-cycle.org

Not only is Exeter's Book-Cycle in a beautiful building – an ancient, half-timbered one full of wonky bookshelves, squishy armchairs and low beams – it's also a pretty beautiful concept. Shoppers can choose up to three secondhand books a day, and decide what they want to pay for them. It's all volunteer-run and the charity also works to provide free books to children and to plant trees with the donated money they make.

237 **BARTER BOOKS**

AT: ALNWICK STATION
Alnwick,
Northumberland
NE66 2NP
North East
+44 (0)16 6560 4888
barterbooks.co.uk

Barter Books is a beautiful and sprawling secondhand and antiquarian bookshop that has taken up home (and increasing amounts of space, over the years) within Alnwick's former train station. Trains stopped calling at the platforms in 1968, but you can still spy lots of the station's original features, as well as a quirky model railway that runs around between bookshelves. Open fires on chilly days and lots of comfy seating make it an appealing place to while away an afternoon.

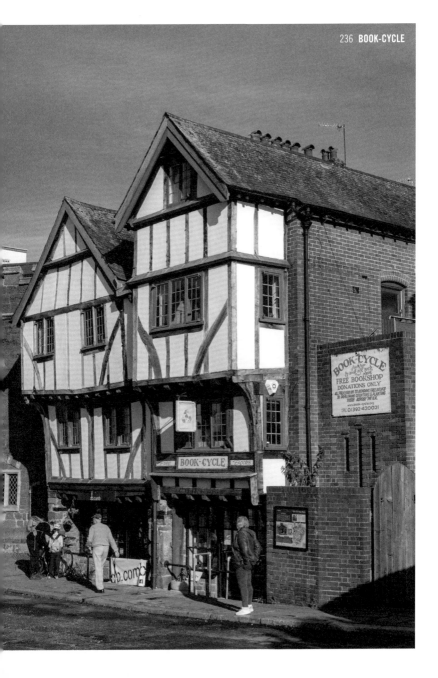

238 PERSEPHONE BOOKS

8 Edgar Buildings
Bath,
Somerset
BA1 2EE
South West
+44 (0)12 2542 5050
*persephone
books.co.uk*

The saying 'don't judge a book by its cover' can be taken quite literally at Persephone, where all the books on the shelves are a matching shade of grey. Each of the 145 books on their shelves are reprints of forgotten-about fiction and non-fiction by (mainly) female writers from the 20th century. They've saved and revived a number of really great reads over the years. Peak inside each book's grey jacket – the endpaper of every Persephone publication is a bold fabric pattern that has a link to the story within.

239 SCARTHIN BOOKS

The Promenade
Cromford,
Derbyshire
DE4 3QF
Central England
+44 (0)16 2982 3272
scarthinbooks.com

You'll find Scarthin Books on a narrow street overlooking a pond in Cromford, on the edge of the Peak District. The much-loved indie has been selling books since 1974. You can pick up new volumes, as well as secondhand and rare books here, plus sheet music and literary-themed gifts. Once you've selected your next tale, settle down in the on-site veggie cafe and get reading.

238 PERSEPHONE BOOKS

240 P&G WELLS

11 College St
Winchester,
Hampshire
SO23 9LZ
South East
+44 (0)19 6285 2016
pgwells.co.uk

Behind Winchester's huge cathedral, you'll find Kingsgate Village, a handful of pretty, historic streets home to Winchester College, a pub and a few small shops. One of them is P&G Wells, a warm, welcoming and well-stocked bookshop that's been selling in the same spot since 1729. Upstairs is crammed full of the best in children's literature, while downstairs is stocked with new releases, bestsellers, non-fiction and work from local authors.

241 DAUNT BOOKS MARYLEBONE

83-84 Marylebone
High St
London
W1U 4QW
South East
+44 (0)20 7224 2295
dauntbooks.co.uk

It may be something of a London institution – Daunt have been selling books in this historic building, as well as a handful of others across the capital, since 1990 – but this gem, a little off the beaten track, still feels like an incredible find each time you visit. The beautiful building opens out to reveal shelf after shelf of carefully curated tomes. Check out the event calendar too for ace readings and talks.

242 MUCH ADO BOOKS

8 West St
Alfriston,
East Sussex
BN26 5UX
South East
+44 (0)13 2387 1222
muchadobooks.com

Much Ado is equal parts as charming as its setting, in the picture-book village of Alfriston. Across two floors and various outbuildings (there's a shepherd's hut filled with secondhand and vintage books), this bookshop wins over book lovers with its selection of hand-picked volumes, notebooks, prints and crafty offerings. Pick up a 'bits kit', full of paper scraps, stamps, postcards, letters and pages from books damaged beyond repair for creating your own bookish collage.

VINTAGE *finds*

243 **THE CONFIT POT**

22 Mermaid St
Rye,
East Sussex
TN31 7ET
South East
+44 (0)17 9722 7333
theconfitpot.com

Pretty Rye has a fitting collection of retro shops to match the town's historic vibe. The Confit Pot is one of the best, stocked with stacks of vintage French interiors, glassware and things for the garden. It also has one of the largest collections of confit pots in the country. These chunky clay pots were used in food preparation and preservation during the 18th and 19th century – and also happen to be rather lovely to look at.

244 **COW MANCHESTER**

61 Church St
Manchester
M4 1PD
North West
+44 (0)16 1834 4926
wearecow.com

Vintage and secondhand fashion are what you visit Cow's stores for, and Manchester's northern quarter outpost is one of the best. Here you'll find vintage clothing from the 1960s, 70s, 80s, 90s, and even the 00s, all displayed in ways that easily inspire your next full outfit. Don't miss Cow's own reworked range, which is made up of current styles created out of outdated vintage pieces and salvaged fabrics.

245 **POSITIVE RETAIL**

26 Addington St
Ramsgate,
Kent
CT11 9JJ
South East
positive-retail.com

Positive Retail sells a perfectly curated collection of premium preloved clothes and deadstock fashion. The aim? Elevate resale to reduce the amount of waste the fashion industry currently creates. The end product is a popular local shop which is a joy to visit – and might just change the way you think about your wardrobe.

246 HUNGERFORD ARCADE

26-27 High St
Hungerford,
Berkshire
RG17 0NF
South East
+44 (0)14 8868 3701
hungerford
arcade.com

A sprawling maze full of treasure to uncover, Hungerford Arcade sells everything from genuinely precious antiques to secondhand slippers, via vintage children's books, china tea sets, retro signage and Victorian chamber pots. You can easily lose half a day browsing (luckily there's a cafe if you need a refuel mid-sweep). Once you've had your fill, check out the rest of Hungerford's high street which boasts a couple of other antique emporiums filled with delights too.

247 69A

75 Renshaw St
Liverpool,
Merseyside
L1 2SJ
North West
+44 (0)15 1708 8873
69aliverpool.co.uk

Confusingly, you'll find 69A at 75 Renshaw Street (the name stuck after the shop moved to a different building on the same street in the late 1980s.) These days, the 19th-century townhouse is stuffed full of collectable curios, from postcards and prints to incredible rare works of art, vintage buttons to stuffed birds – treasures worth pocket change to serious investments.

248 WOLF & GYPSY VINTAGE

30 Sydney St
Brighton,
East Sussex
BN1 4EP
South East
+44 (0)12 7367 1797
wolfandgypsy
vintage.co.uk

Stylish secondhand garb sits alongside new stock from eco-conscious labels at Brighton's Wolf & Gypsy Vintage. This is the place to pick up an antique cotton nightdress, a 1990s silk skirt and a glass bottle of cruelty-free, vegan face serum in one turn around the spacious and thoughtfully laid-out shop.

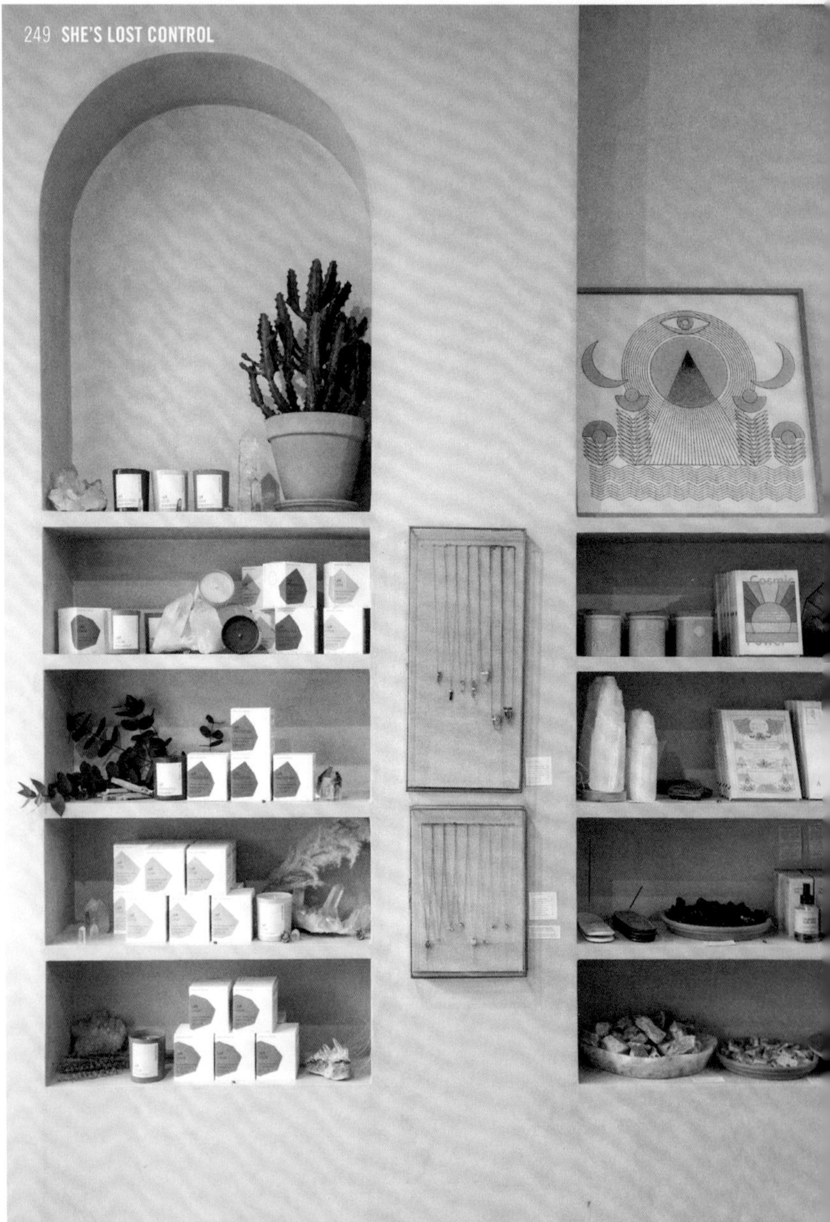

Unique **BOUTIQUES**

249 SHE'S LOST CONTROL

74 Broadway Market
London
E8 4QJ
South East
+44 (0)20 3196 7690
sheslostcontrol.co.uk

Need somewhere to stock up on ethical crystals, or just curious about the whole alternative wellness scene? She's Lost Control is the place to go for unusual beauty products, oracle and tarot cards, spells and candles. They are also big supporters of the crystal mining community, and promote responsibly sourced and mined gems with transparent supply chains. The shop runs a series of events too, so stop by if you fancy getting your aura photographed and your cards read, or if your frazzled soul could do with a spot of sound healing, candlelit yoga or the connection of a sharing circle.

250 HAECKELS

18 Cliff Terrace
Margate,
Kent
CT9 1RU
South East
+44 (0)12 2720 3675
haeckels.co.uk

Handpicked Margate seaweed is the starting point for Haeckels' dreamy skin care, which is all sold in recyclable or compostable packaging. Where better to buy it than at their flagship store, metres from where that seaweed is harvested? Elevate your visit with a treatment, like a seaweed bath with a sea view, or a steamy spell inside Haeckels' nearby sea bathing machine: a community-run, donation-based sauna sat right next to the sea.

251 SANCHO'S

117 Fore St
Exeter,
Devon
EX4 3JQ
South West
+44 (0)13 9275 7510
sanchosshop.com

Sancho's is one special shop. It's a Black-owned, sustainable store, selling gifts, homewares and fashion, where you can be sure everything has been handpicked for a good reason. They only stock high-quality products made from organic, recycled or recyclable materials – and they prioritise size-inclusive brands. It's ethical shopping made effortless.

252 RE

Bishops Yard
Corbridge,
Northumberland
NE45 5LA
North East
+44 (0)14 3463 4567
re-foundobjects.com

Stock is eclectic and ever changing at RE, an old industrial unit turned shoppers treasure trove. But you can be sure everything on sale here is either 'rare, remarkable, recycled, rescued or restored'. The aim is for it to be fair trade and environmentally friendly too. You can pick up anything from cheese grater candle holders and hand-painted tin cans to party hats made in rural Bangladesh out of old newspapers, via 1930s lemonade jugs and vintage Christmas tree decorations.

253 OBJECTS OF USE

AT: 6 LINCOLN HOUSE
Market St
Oxford,
Oxfordshire
OX1 3EQ
South East
+44 (0)18 6524 1705
objectsofuse.com

Hardware stores might not usually inspire delight, but this one is pretty much guaranteed to. Its neat shelves are stocked with simple and traditional everyday objects made from natural materials and sourced from around the world. Stop by to stock up on hand-dipped beeswax candles, enamel milk jugs, linen tea towels, ostrich feather dusters, beautifully boxed soap and the kind of stylish, handcrafted tools you won't want to leave to get dusty in the shed.

254 DOMESTIC SCIENCE

53 Long St
Tetbury,
Gloucestershire
GL8 8AA
South West
+44 (0)16 6650 3667
domesticscience
home.co.uk

All four floors of this Georgian townhouse are filled with treats. Domestic Science sells a clever mix of aesthetically pleasing vintage and contemporary homewares, plus some fashion and a nice line in cute kids' toys. Go for a vintage galvanised watering can, leave weighed down by soft throws, felt slippers and pretty notebooks.

255 PRIOR

AT: CABOT CIRCUS
23 Philadelphia St
Bristol
BS1 3BZ
South West
+44 (0)73 9381 9558
priorshop.uk

Prior aims to challenge our fast fashion shopping habits, selling a curated collection of thoughtful items created by (largely local) sustainable designers. You'll find things like hand-knitted socks, small batch vegan bath bombs and easy womenswear in soft, natural fabrics. You can also pick up DIY kits if you want to try your own hand at something creative, while their central Bristol shop hosts welcoming workshops on subjects like candle making and lino printing.

F A R M *shops*

256 **COBBS FARM SHOP**

Bath Road
Hungerford,
Berkshire
RG17 0SP
South East
+44 (0)14 8850 8445
cobbsfarmshops.co.uk

Cobbs' Hungerford shop is surrounded by their neat 55-acre farm. Inside, fresh veg plucked straight from the fields sits alongside local produce. You'll also find fresh bread, delicious deli counter delights, a fishmonger and butchers, and shelves of snacks, preserves and appealing store cupboard ingredients. Try before you buy at their on-site cafe. There's another, slightly more raucous, one next to the farm's play barn, if you have little kids in tow.

257 **HARTLEY FARM SHOP AND KITCHEN**

Winsley,
Wiltshire
BA15 2JB
South West
+44 (0)12 2586 4948
hartley-farm.co.uk

Five generations of the Bowles family have farmed land in Winsley, but recently the 125-acre farm has changed tact. Following regenerative practices, the farm is now home to a herd of native-breed cattle, a small flock of hens, beehives, fruit orchards and an organic market garden, all of which supply Hartley Farm Shop and Kitchen. The farm shop is a cornucopia of fresh produce and pantry fare. Whatever isn't grown or produced on the Bowles' farm is sourced as locally as possible.

258 **TEBAY SERVICES**

AT: WESTMORLAND
PLACE
Orton,
Cumbria
CA10 3SB
North West
tebayservices.com

Motorway service stations are usually necessities rather than destinations in themselves, but then most service stations aren't like Tebay Services. Tebay is owned by the local Dunning family. They opened it in 1972 after the M6 motorway was built through their farm. You can fill up your tank here, beside the M6, and then you can also pick up locally sourced treats from the farm shop. We're talking fresh produce, an impressive cheese counter, and a proper butchers selling fresh cuts of meat, hand-pressed burgers and pies made from beef raised on the Dunning farm, which still surrounds the services. In a rush? The Quick Kitchen is open 24 hours a day, if you just need to grab a sausage roll and a coffee to go. If you've got time, linger for a meal. You can even get a stellar roast lunch here on a Sunday.

THE RIVERFORD FIELD KITCHEN

FOOD and DRINK 🍴

Restaurants in
UNUSUAL LOCATIONS

259 THE TREEHOUSE RESTAURANT

AT: THE ALNWICK GARDEN

**Denwick Lane
Alnwick,
Northumberland
NE66 1YU
North East
+44 (0)16 6551 1350**
alnwickgarden.com

Twinkling lights and twiggy interiors greet diners at The Treehouse Restaurant, a wooden restaurant that, you guessed it, is high above the ground. Said to be the largest wooden treehouse in the world, it's built around 16 lime trees, which grow through the restaurant itself. The food is hearty and traditional, but really, you're here for the surreal setting.

259 THE TREEHOUSE RESTAURANT

260 FALLING FOSS TEA GARDEN

Foss Lane
Near Littlebeck,
North Yorkshire
YO22 5JD
North East
+44 (0)77 2347 7929
*fallingfoss
teagarden.co.uk*

Surrounded by ancient woodland, a couple of minutes from a stunning, secluded waterfall (Falling Foss itself), this alfresco cafe is all kinds of charming. Open daily during the summer months and for the odd weekend during the winter, Falling Foss Tea Garden is an otherworldly spot to pause in the forest. Combine with a walk through the trees to work up an appetite and then grab a table outside among the greenery for cake and coffee or a cup of warming soup. There are umbrellas to keep you dry if the weather isn't kind when you visit.

261 THE RIVERFORD FIELD KITCHEN

AT: WASH FARM
Buckfastleigh,
Devon
TQ11 0JU
South West
+44 (0)18 0322 7391
*fieldkitchen.
riverford.co.uk*

Riverford are the producers of ethical vegetable boxes that they deliver around the country. Visit their original organic farm on the edge of Dartmoor in Devon, and you'll be treated to a veg-centric feast. There's just one sitting in their on-site dining room, where the walls are decorated with colourful dried flowers grown on the farm. Everyone eats at the same time, and mixes together on sharing tables. Meat is on the menu but it's far from the star. Instead bowls of wonderful heritage veggies prepared in creative ways appear one by one at the table. Make sure to save room for dessert – a selection of treats will be laid out beside the kitchen after the main meal.

262 RIVER EXE CAFÉ

Exe Estuary
(by boat from
Exmouth Marina),
Devon
EX8 1FE
South West
+44 (0)77 6111 6103
riverexecafe.com

Constructed in 2011 using two flatbed barges and a shed, River Exe Café is one unusual restaurant. It's floating right in the middle of the River Exe Estuary. Access is by boat only – either you rock up on your own vessel or catch a 25-minute water taxi from Exmouth Marina (it's booked automatically when you reserve a table on board). The covered cafe is tethered, so you won't get seasick or drift off anywhere unexpected during your meal but you will get a unique watery perspective of the Devon coastline from all angles. It may be a little hard to reach, but everyone is catered for irrespective of their mobility needs. Babies, children and dogs are welcome too. Food is local and the focus is on seafood – oysters from Teignmouth and mussels from the River Teign, swimming in Devon Bays beer, all from just along the coast.

263 RYE BAKERY

Whittox Lane
Frome,
Somerset
BA11 3BY
South West
+44 (0)79 2583 0852
rye-bakery.com

Come to Rye Bakery in Frome for their great coffee, flaky pastries, cinnamon buns and epic cheese toasties. Stay for the stunning surroundings. The space they occupy on Whittox Lane is inside a former church which dates back to the early 1800s. Tables are on the ground floor, with a double height ceiling revealing a beautiful organ and stepped seating above. There's also a huge 'nest' woven out of wood at the back of the space, designed to provide customers with a little quiet for breastfeeding.

T I N Y *pubs*

---

264 **THE NUTSHELL**

**The Traverse
Bury St Edmunds,
Suffolk
IP33 1BJ
East of England
+44 (0)12 8476 4867
*thenutshellpub.co.uk***

The smallest pub in England, the diminutive Nutshell has a bar that measures just 15 by 7 feet (4,6 × 2,1 metres). The dinky pub, which has been serving punters since 1867, still manages to pack in an impressive amount of character. Visitors will find a mummified cat, a plane propeller and various taxidermied animals on the walls, while the pub's ceiling is plastered in banknotes from around the world.

264 **THE NUTSHELL**

265 HOUSE OF THE TREMBLING MADNESS

42 Stonegate
York,
North Yorkshire
YO1 8AS
North East
+44 (0)19 0464 0009
trembling
madness.co.uk

You'll find House of the Trembling Madness' tiny bar hidden above their bottle shop on York's Stonegate street. The intimate space is in an old building – it's said to date back to 1180 AD – with a vaulted beam ceiling and loads of atmosphere. Seating is limited but the beer menu certainly isn't. Go prepared to cosy up to strangers and make new friends over a pint. Food is also served all day to accompany the inevitable flow of drinks.

266 THE SIGNAL BOX INN

AT: LAKESIDE STATION
Kings Road
Cleethorpes,
Lincolnshire
DN35 0AG
Central England
+44 (0)14 7260 4657
cclr.co.uk

A signal box at Cleethorpes' light railway station might just be the teeniest pub on the planet. The entire venue, which boasts a regularly changing beer, cider and wine menu, is just 8 by 8 feet (2,5 × 2,5 metres) in size. It's located in a genuine signal box, it just happens to be smaller than usual to reflect the size of the light railway. You can only fit around six people inside before it starts to feel crowded, but there are lots more benches outside for fair weather days.

DISTILLERIES *to visit*

267 **SIPSMITH**

83 Cranbrook Road
Chiswick,
London
W4 2LJ
South East
+44 (0)20 8747 0753
sipsmith.com

Sipsmith's distillery, hidden away on a residential street in West London, is open for tours and tastings on weeknight evenings. You can learn about the history of London gin (spoiler: it's colourful), and of the Sipsmith brand, get up close to their copper stills and taste all their small batch classics, as well as some of their more experimental flavours. You'll also get an amazing G&T to sip throughout the evening.

268 **CONKER DISTILLERY**

Unit 2,
163 Stourvale Road
Bournemouth,
Dorset
BH6 5HQ
South West
+44 (0)12 0243 0384
conkerspirit.co.uk

The home of Conker, a small batch craft distillery producing gins, alcohol-free spirits, coffee liqueurs and pre-mixed cocktails, is a quiet Bournemouth suburb. Visitors can tour the unit to discover Conker's story and the process behind each of their offerings before taking part in a tasting led by their head distiller. If you prefer to make a beeline for the bar – no judgement here – visit when the Distillery Door Tap Room is open to the public (currently every other Friday) to sample creative cocktails in their on-site bar.

269 FISHERS GIN

Crag Path
Aldeburgh,
Suffolk
IP15 5BT
East of England
+44 (0)17 2845 4201
fishersgin.com

Sea views with a side of coastal-inspired gin? Yes, please. Fishers' distillery couldn't be in a more picturesque spot, perched right on the edge of Aldeburgh beach. You can meet their still before taking part in a tutored tasting to see if you can identify any of the unusual coastal plants, like bog myrtle and rock samphire, used to flavour their spirit.

270 BOMBAY SAPPHIRE DISTILLERY

AT: LAVERSTOKE MILL
London Road
Laverstoke,
Hampshire
RG28 7NR
South East
bombaysapphire.com

Tucked away in a rural corner of Hampshire, you'll find the Bombay Sapphire gin distillery in a beautiful and historic setting. The Laverstoke Mill is recorded in the *Domesday Book* of 1086 and was known for manufacturing banknotes in the 18th century. The gin company, which was founded in the early 19th century, moved into the premises in 2010. Now gin stills and an expansive visitor experience fill the elegant old buildings, which sit beside the pretty River Test. Don't miss the glasshouses, a sleek modern addition filled with the plants and botanicals that go into a bottle of Bombay Sapphire.

Cool **BREWERIES**

---

271 **THE FLOWER POTS BREWERY**
Brandy Mount /
Westfield Road
Cheriton,
Hampshire
SO24 0QQ
South East
+44 (0)19 6277 1735
theflowerpots.co.uk

Much-loved village pub The Flower Pots Inn has been brewing its own beer since the 1850s. It all happens on site, next to the pub and its meadow which becomes a buzzy beer garden on summer days. The brewery itself isn't open for tours, but you can buy beers – by the bottle, jug or cask – straight from the source here. Before you make your selection, it's wise to try them out at the pub. You won't find a fresher serve.

272 **BREW YORK**
AT: UNIT 6,
ENTERPRISE COMPLEX
York,
North Yorkshire
YO1 9TT
North East
+44 (0)19 0484 8448
brewyork.co.uk

Tucked away beside the River Foss, within York's historic walls, you'll find Brew York's original outpost. The brand, which was founded by two pals in 2016, brews all their beers in the city of York, a lot of it here where you'll also find a taproom and beer hall for sampling pints. Take a tour and learn about the process before settling down for a drink or two in the open plan space which is shared with the tanks themselves.

273 WIPER AND TRUE OLD MARKET

AT: UNIT 11,
CITY BUSINESS PARK
Easton Road
Bristol
BS5 0SP
South West
+44 (0)11 7941 2501
wiperandtrue.com

This Bristol-based brewers has two sites in the city. After outgrowing their original in St Werburghs, they opened a second brewery and taproom in 2022. It's a beautiful light-filled space that aims to be welcoming, inclusive and accessible, with a big focus on great beer, obviously. The Wiper and True Old Market Taproom serves their trademark craft beers as well as local natural wines, cocktails and spirits plus alcohol-free options – and food from Bristol-based Japanese restaurant Eatchu. You'll also find events like bookable brewery tours, markets, yoga classes and creative workshops being put on here too.

273 WIPER AND TRUE OLD MARKET

274 **ADNAMS**

Victoria St
Southwold,
Suffolk
IP18 6JW
East of England
+44 (0)15 0272 7200
adnams.co.uk

Beer has a long history in Southwold. According to Adnams, it's been brewed on the same site in town for nearly 700 years. The brand itself was established in 1890, and now dominates drinks lists in the local pubs and restaurants, many of which are run by Adnams too. You can go behind the scenes at their historic brewery in the heart of the seaside town before ending up in the tasting bar for a pint of Ghost Ship. Fan of the stronger stuff too? Adnams also produce vodka, gin and whisky at their Suffolk home and you can tour their distillery too.

275 **CLOUDWATER BREW CO.**

7-8 Piccadilly
Trading Estate
Manchester
M1 2NP
North West
+44 (0)16 1661 5943
cloudwaterbrew.co

Cloudwater brew and package all their beers in Manchester. You can get up close to their modern brewery, and get as deep into the technical stuff as takes your fancy, on a tour of the site. Next door, check out their Unit 9 taproom for a choice of super-fresh pints pulled from 20 draft taps. You can also buy bottles and cans of your faves to take away.

English **VINEYARDS**

276 **TINWOOD ESTATE**
AT: TINWOOD FARM
Halnaker,
West Sussex
PO18 0NE
South East
+44 (0)12 4353 7372
tinwoodestate.com

Tucked away on the outskirts of Chichester, Tinwood was transformed from arable farm to vineyard by owner Art Tukker when he took over from his parents. It's now a small, successful sparkling wine vineyard offering tours and tastings in a pretty light-filled space surrounded by vines. Pimp your tasting with a cheese board or afternoon tea, and make sure you don't leave without a bottle of Tinwood's sparkling rosé under your arm.

277 **KINSBROOK VINEYARD**
West Chiltington
Road
Thakeham,
West Sussex
RH20 2RZ
South East
+44 (0)14 0390 7800
kinsbrook
vineyard.com

A newcomer to the English wine scene, Kinsbrook planted their first vines in 2017. Tours of their 56.000 vines, as well as wine tastings, are available. You can also just rock up and soak up the site for yourself. Kinsbrook Farmhouse is home to a farm shop and eatery, serving a simple menu made up of locally sourced treats.

278 TILLINGHAM

AT: DEW FARM

**Dew Lane
Peasmarsh,
East Sussex
TN31 6XD
South East
+44 (0)17 9720 8226**
tillingham.com

Grapes aren't the only thing you'll find at Tillingham. As well as vineyards, the secluded farm has fruit trees, ancient woodland, livestock, accommodation and a bar and two restaurants, serving up great local ingredients (and glasses of Tillingham natural wine) in very cool settings. The hub of the estate is the coming together of old and new: traditional oast house architecture, sleek modern farm buildings and a converted dutch barn where you can eat wood-fired sourdough pizzas alfresco. You can take tours of the vines, which run across some of the farm's 70 acres, and take part in a guided tasting of a handful of Tillingham vinos. Follow up with more samples at the bar (admiring Tillingham's wine bottle labels), then dinner, and even a night on the farm if you can't tear yourself away.

279 RYEDALE

AT: FARFIELD FARM
Westow,
North Yorkshire
YO60 7LS
North East
+44 (0)16 5365 8035
ryedalevineyards.co.uk

Most of England's vineyards are found in the south, especially around East and West Sussex and Kent where the soil and climate conditions are closest to those in France. But that doesn't mean you can't grow grapes further north. Ryedale is one of the most northerly commercial vineyards in England. They have 12 acres of vines, which you can explore alongside their on-site winery. Don't leave without trying their Strickland Red – it's an award winner.

280 CASTLEWOOD VINEYARD

Musbury
Devon
EX13 8SS
South West
+44 (0)78 1255 4861
castlewood
vineyard.co.uk

Pretty Castlewood is on a hilly farm in rural Devon, where the Corbett family grow and produce sparkling and still wines on a small scale, as naturally as possible. If you're part of a group of six or more, you can arrange a private tour and tasting at Castlewood, while their cellar door is open all the time if you'd like to swing by the farm and pick up a case or two.

B E A C H *cafes*

281 OSBORNE BROS
High St
Leigh-on-Sea,
Essex
SS9 2ER
East of England
+44 (0)17 0247 7233
osbornebros.co.uk

Perched besides the River Thames estuary as it flows out into the sea, Osborne Bros has been selling fish and shellfish since 1880. The original 19th-century cockle sheds are located nearby, where their fishmonger and cockle processing factory are still based, though you can also sample their fare from a cafe in an 18th-century stable mews next to the water. Grab a bench outside to sample traditional snacks like cockles, jellied eels, shrimp, whelks and winkles, or dressed crab and crayfish sandwiches.

282 BEACHHOUSE
South Milton
Devon
TQ7 3JY
South West
+44 (0)15 4856 1144
beachhousedevon.com

On the South West Coast Path at the edge of South Milton Sands, Beachhouse has gold-standard views of the sea. It's open year round and makes a cosy shelter from the elements in winter (especially with a boozy hot chocolate in hand), with alfresco tables in an unbeatable spot for sunnier days. Expect enticing small plates and incredible seafood feasts as well as toasties, sandwiches and soups if you're after a simpler meal.

283 THE HIDDEN HUT

**Porthcurnick
Beach
Cornwall
TR2 5EW
South West**
hiddenhut.co.uk

Snack shack by day, organiser of magical beach feasts by night, The Hidden Hut is one dreamy discovery. The open-air eatery is tucked away on a secluded stretch of the Cornish coastal path between Portscatho and St Mawes. Open year round, it serves up delicious takeaway lunches (Cornish pasties, cakes, chowders, dhals and enormous salads) to be enjoyed on Porthcurnick Beach. But things get really special during the summer when The Hut puts on beach feast nights. Lucky diners (you need to secure your spot in advance) are served one spectacular themed dish to be consumed on the sand. When the tide is especially low, that means long communal tables on the beach. You bring your own plate, cutlery and booze (plus whatever you need to brave chilly or rainy Cornish evenings) and The Hidden Hut chefs provide the flavours. Previous themes have included Champagne Shells, Summer Sardines, Lobster & Chips and an epic veggie South Indian Thali feast.

284 RILEY'S FISH SHACK

**King Edward's Bay
Tynemouth,
Tyne and Wear
NE30 4BY
North East
+44 (0)19 1257 1371**
rileysfishshack.com

Two converted shipping containers down on the sand at King Edward's Bay, beneath the imposing ruins of Tynemouth Priory and Castle, house Riley's Fish Shack. It's a buzzy beach front cafe serving up fresh, simple fare, cooked over a BBQ grill and elevated by clever flavour combos. Right beside the North Sea, Riley's braves the elements and stays open all year round. The menu changes regularly, depending on what's available from the local daily catch.

285 THE HUT

Colwell Bay
Isle of Wight
PO40 9NP
South East
+44 (0)19 8389 8637
thehutcolwell.co.uk

On a warm day, you can believe you're eating besides the clear blue waters of the Med at The Hut. Instead, you'll be overlooking the English Channel from Colwell Bay on the Isle of Wight. It's a mega spot for sipping a chilled white and feasting on plates of fresh grilled fish, seafood curries or surf and turf. Take the day to explore the rest of the island, or just swing by for lunch via passenger ferry from Lymington to Yarmouth, which is nearby. Have your own boat? Ribs and small boats can anchor off the front of the restaurant.

286 WATCH HOUSE CAFÉ

East Beach
West Bay,
Dorset
DT6 4EN
South West
+44 (0)13 0845 9330
watchhousecafe.co.uk

On the stones of West Bay's beach, with uninterrupted views of the sea and the golden cliffs rising up to the east, sits Watch House Café. You can take away and sit on the shingle, soak up some vitamin D from the outside terrace or, on colder days, grab a table inside. Choose from classics like fish and chips and crab sandwiches, or try one of the cafe's trademark wood-fired pizzas.

287 GOAT LEDGE

Warrior Square –
Lower Promenade
St Leonards on Sea,
East Sussex
TN37 6FA
South East
goatledge.com

A little shack on St Leonards seafront, with a handful of flamboyantly decorated beach huts you can book to eat and drink in, Goat Ledge is open for breakfast, lunch, dinner and sunset drinks. Drop by for a smoked haddock bap to start the day, or end it with *moules marinières* and a half of local ale right on the stones, sound tracked by live music if you're lucky.

288 BILLY'S ON THE BEACH

**Bracklesham Lane
Bracklesham Bay,
West Sussex
PO20 8JH
South East
+44 (0)12 4367 0373**
*billyson
thebeach.co.uk*

You can see the English Channel, passing boats and, on a clear day, the Isle of Wight from a table at Billy's. It's positioned just behind the sea wall near the Witterings, a stretch of southern coastline that's populated with bold beachfront homes as well as simple 1960s constructions and shops selling traditional sweets, piping hot fish and chips and all the things you need to become a convincing surfer. Open year round, Billy's is a surprisingly lovely spot from which to enjoy sea views and dishes like *moules frites*, smoked mackerel pâté and whole fresh dressed crab.

287 GOAT LEDGE

The OLDEST PUBS in England

289 THE ROYAL STANDARD OF ENGLAND

**Brindle Lane
Forty Green,
Buckinghamshire
HP9 1XT
South East
+44 (0)14 9467 3382**
theoldestpub.com

The Royal Standard has been welcoming visitors for over 900 years, and calls itself the oldest free house in England. Step inside and you'll be greeted by dark wooden beams, well-worn medieval floors and the lingering smell of wood smoke. It really feels like you leave the modern world outside the front door, and that's even before you hear rumours of the many ghosts that allegedly haunt the boozer. The traditional pub atmosphere extends to the menu, which is populated with fancy takes on hearty English comfort food like Scotch eggs, sausages and mash, handmade pies and Sunday roasts. Leave room for apple pie, spotted dick or a steamed sponge pudding with warm custard for dessert.

290 THE PORCH HOUSE

Digbeth St
Stow-on-the-Wold,
Gloucestershire
GL54 1BN
South West
+44 (0)14 5187 0048
porch-house.co.uk

A cosy, quintessentially Cotswolds pub in Stow-on-the-Wold, The Porch House purports to be England's oldest inn. Parts of the building, namely wooden beams which were recently carbon-dated, hail from around 1000 BC, though the majority of what you see today dates back from the 16th and 17th centuries. Look out for witch marks above the fireplace, put there to ward off evil spirits. And for those low door frames, if you don't want to bump your head.

291 OLD FERRY BOAT

Holywell,
Cambridgeshire
PE27 4TG
East of England
+44 (0)14 8046 3227
greeneking-pubs.co.uk

A white, thatched inn overlooking the River Ouse, Old Ferry Boat is another boozer that lays claim to being the oldest pub in England. Records show drinks being sold here in 560 AD. Things have changed a fair bit over the years – it's now run by brewery Greene King and has been modernised inside – but a seat beside the fire here remains an appealing spot in which to sip a pint.

Pints with **DREAMY VIEWS**

---

292 **THE OLD NEPTUNE**

Marine Terrace
Whitstable,
Kent
CT5 1EJ
South East
+44 (0)12 2727 2262
thepubon
thebeach.co.uk

The Old Neptune, or 'The Neppy' as it's also known, is right on the stones of Whitstable Beach. It's beyond the sea wall with nothing between it and the breaking waves (a fact which resulted in it being almost completely washed away by a bad storm in the 19th century). On a mild day, drinkers can sit on picnic benches on the beach, while chillier days call for pints sipped inside beside the window, with incredible views of the sea just the other side of the glass.

292 **THE OLD NEPTUNE**

293 THE DRUNKEN DUCK INN

293 THE DRUNKEN DUCK INN

Barngates,
Cumbria
LA22 0NG
North West
+44 (0)15 3943 6347
*drunkenduck
inn.co.uk*

To nab the best table at The Drunken Duck Inn, a charming boozer on a rural crossroads in the Lake District, you need to head out of the pub, cross the road and settle down at one of the handful of benches on the grassy verge. From here a view of fields tumbling down into a valley with purple peaks as the backdrop will accompany your pint of Barngates Brewery Cat Nap, which is brewed behind the pub. The food here is stellar too. When the light fades, head inside for a hearty feast.

294 THE TROUT INN

195 Godstow Road
Oxford,
Oxfordshire
OX2 8PN
South East
+44 (0)18 6551 0930
thetroutoxford.co.uk

This 17th-century Oxford watering hole, perched right on the edge of the River Thames as it flows through Port Meadow, has the kind of outdoor space beer garden dreams are made of. Tables run alongside the water, with ace views of grand Godstow Bridge, the flowing river and any passing wildlife.

295 THE SHEPPEY

Lower Godney,
Somerset
BA5 1RZ
South West
+44 (0)14 5883 1594
thesheppey.co.uk

A little unassuming from the outside, The Sheppey opens up to show off a seriously dreamy vista, thanks to its isolated location. It's right in the middle of the watery Somerset Levels surrounded by farmland and peat moors. A pint of local cider is best enjoyed on The Sheppey's outdoor terrace, which hangs over the River Sheppey. But big, floor-to-ceiling windows mean you can get a good view from inside too. Hang around once the sun sets – this pub is also known for its live music.

296 THE ANCHOR INN

Seatown,
Dorset
DT6 6JU
South West
+44 (0)12 9748 9215
theanchorinn
seatown.co.uk

The Anchor sits at the edge of the sea, with just a handful of houses and some static caravans for company. The South West Coast Path, which links up coastal footpaths in Dorset, Devon, Cornwall and Somerset, passes right in front of the pub, making it a great stopoff on a ramble around this part of the Jurassic coastline. Grab one of the benches in the beer garden, which buts up against the beach but from a vantage point that promises ace views of the sea and Seatown Beach's chunky cliffs.

297 THE SALTHOUSE DUN COW

Purdy St
Salthouse,
Norfolk
NR25 7XA
East of England
+44 (0)12 6374 0870
salthouseduncow.com

From your spot in the sizeable garden of The Salthouse Dun Cow, there's nothing between you and the north Norfolk coastline. Salt marshes simply stretch away into the smooth horizon until they meet the sea. When you've finished your pint, visit Cookie's Crab Shop just around the corner and pick up some fresh crab sandwiches to munch on Salthouse Beach.

F O O D I E *destinations*

298 **COOMBESHEAD FARM**
Lewannick,
Cornwall
PL15 7QQ
South West
coombeshead
farm.co.uk

The handful of tables at Coombeshead book up quickly, sometimes months in advance (bookings open for Sunday lunch here six months ahead of time). The majority of what you find on the menu comes from the working farm, 66 acres of isolated Cornish countryside. They keep pigs, sheep, cows, chickens and ducks, as well as growing (and preserving) vegetables and fruit, while the on-site bakery provides the restaurant with incredible loaves baked from heritage grains. Each meal is a set menu, shifting with the seasons and what the farm offers up. Fallen totally in love with the place? There's also a guesthouse if you want to immerse yourself in Coombeshead life, though you'll want to book that pretty far in advance too.

299 **HARTNETT HOLDER & CO**
AT: LIME WOOD HOTEL
Beaulieu Road
Lyndhurst,
Hampshire
SO43 7FZ
South East
+44 (0)23 8028 7177
limewoodhotel.co.uk

For a relaxed yet fancy vibe, try Hartnett Holder & Co. It's set within Lime Wood Hotel, a country house hotel surrounded by the scenery of the New Forest. The menu has an Italian influence, featuring clever and comforting flavours that reflect the seasons changing outside the window. Whatever time of year you visit, you can be sure to find plates of perfect hand-rolled pasta and delightful boozy desserts.

300 THE SPORTSMAN

Faversham Road
Seasalter,
Kent
CT5 4BP
South East
+44 (0)12 2727 3370
thesportsman
seasalter.co.uk

This understated beach-front restaurant might, at first impression, seem like an unlikely dining destination. But one bite of heavenly bread paired with hand-churned butter and Seasalter salt and you'll be more than convinced. The Sportsman serves up one seasonal and locally sourced five-course tasting menu with a little variation you can choose from on the day (though worth noting they don't cater to vegan or dairy-free diners). Being so close to the sea, you'll find rock oysters, crab and seaweed often feature on the menu. It's about an hour's walk along the coast from Whitstable if you fancy arriving by foot and working up a solid appetite before lunch.

301 L'ENCLUME

Cavendish St
Cartmel,
Cumbria
LA11 6QA
North West
+44 (0)15 3953 6362
lenclume.co.uk

Cartmel is not exactly the kind of place you expect to stumble across a restaurant boasting three Michelin stars. But the tiny village which straddles the River Eea on the edge of the Lake District is home to L'Enclume, a gold-standard dining destination where food is sustainable (they have a green Michelin star too), experimental and borderline transcendental. Little Cartmel is also known for its take on the classic English dessert, the sticky toffee pudding. Pick one up from the Village Shop, if you have any room left after your feast at L'Enclume (unlikely.)

302 PINE

AT: VALLUM FARM
Military Road
East Wallhouses,
Northumberland
NE18 0LL
North East
+44 (0)14 3467 1202
restaurantpine.co.uk

You'll find Pine in an old cow barn in rural Northumberland, where, amazingly, tables overlook sections of Hadrian's Wall. Ingredients are grown on site, foraged from the surrounding, plentiful countryside or sourced as locally as possible. Guests settle down for around three hours of feasting in the evenings, when Pine serves an extensive tasting menu full of intriguing flavour combinations, like lobster, fermented strawberry and pine.

303 PENSONS

AT: NETHERWOOD
ESTATE
**Tenbury Wells,
Worcestershire
WR15 8RT
Central England
+44 (0)18 8541 0333**
pensons.co.uk

Pensons is another English restaurant which holds a Michelin green star for sustainability, thanks to its focus on hyper-local ingredients, many of which are foraged or grown on the estate. Diners are welcomed to try dishes from an à la carte lunch menu or evening tasting menu in a beautiful old converted barn in a rural spot by the Herefordshire-Worcestershire border. Arrive early to wander through the kitchen gardens before your meal – you may well spot an ingredient that'll turn up on your plate moments later.

304 SILO

AT: UNIT 7,
QUEENS YARD
**Hackney Wick,
London
E9 5EN
South East
+44 (0)20 7993 8155**
silolondon.com

A lot of thought goes into what goes in the bin – as well as onto the plates – at Silo in East London. It's a zero-waste restaurant. Silo chefs make as much as they can from scratch, only allowing products to be delivered to the restaurant in reusable containers. That means any waste that is created by the kitchen is compostable. It also means the menu is a little unusual. They recently ran a series of special suppers inspired by invasive species, where Japanese knotweed and jellyfish made the menu. On an average day, you can sample dishes like fallow deer, celeriac and quince or go all-in and eat your way through everything like a tasting menu. Delicious and virtuous.

LOST MEADOW TREEPOD

SLEEP ☾

Secluded **CAMPSITES**

305 **FRY'S WOOD**

AT: CAMPWELL FARM
Winsley,
Wiltshire
BA15 2JH
South West
+44 (0)12 2558 2246
campwell.co.uk

Drive over bumpy farm tracks until you feel like you've missed the signs, park up and there's still a little walk through shrubbery and new woodland until you spot your home for the night: big bell tents, complete with proper comfy beds and wood burners to take the chill off. Fry's Wood is ideal for a big group camping together – there's a number of communal areas like a partially alfresco kitchen, a covered dining area with pizza oven and a big firepit – but there's also room around each tent for a pleasing level of privacy. Wake up slowly with a cup of tea in the ancient bluebell woodland which edges the site before taking a hot shower. It's open to the elements with tree branches bobbing overhead. Heaven.

306 **CAMP KÁTUR**

AT: THE CAMP HILL
ESTATE
Kirklington,
North Yorkshire
DL8 2LS
North East
+44 (0)18 4520 2100
campkatur.com

Wake with the sunrise and stargaze late into the night in one of Camp Kátur's geodomes, which are dotted around their estate in meadows and wooded glades. Some have log burners, hot tubs and private kitchens, while others are totally off-grid for a more back-to-nature experience. After a unique adventure? Book the Secret Hide Unidome. Hidden away in dense woodland, the dome is totally clear for unobstructed views of the greenery which surrounds you while you sleep.

307 **WOODFIRE**

AT: WESTERLANDS
ESTATE
Graffham,
West Sussex
GU28 0QJ
South East
+44 (0)17 9832 0021
woodfire.co.uk

You can pitch your own tent or borrow a beautiful vintage one at Woodfire's Westerlands location. You'll be snoozing in the heart of the South Downs National Park, just a little north of the South Downs Way, a walking route which takes you from Winchester to Eastbourne via some of the South of England's loveliest landscapes. Expect big views and big skies at this quiet rural spot, but don't go assuming there is nothing going on here. Each weekend, Woodfire staff cook up delicious feasts over an open fire (ideal if your DIY camping skills aren't up to much) where you can dig in to warming stews or grilled dishes for dinner, and hot bacon and egg sandwiches for breakfast, all eaten outdoors around communal tables.

306 **CAMP KÁTUR**

D R E A M Y *hotels*

308 THE ROSE

91 High St
Deal,
Kent
CT14 6ED
South East
+44 (0)13 0438 9127
therosedeal.com

An unassuming pub set back from the seafront in Deal, The Rose hides eight beautiful and unique rooms behind a thick velvet curtain at the bottom of the stairs. While downstairs, guests enjoy a surprising, modern menu on vintage crockery in the eclectic dining room, upstairs you'll find bold colours, retro prints and dreamy velvet headboards. All the richly decorated rooms are a welcome retreat from the everyday, but Room 1's soft pink tones and floral accents and Room 6, with its arty vibes, are especially lovely.

309 THE PIG AT HARLYN BAY

Harlyn,
Cornwall
PL28 8SQ
South West
+44 (0)34 5225 9494
thepighotel.com

Set back from the village which has grown up around Harlyn Bay, The Pig's Cornish outpost is a grand manor house which dates back to the 15th century. The hotel is a short walk down to the sand, yet also feels like it's in its own little bubble, surrounded by open space as well as The Pig's trademark kitchen garden. Have a drink by the fire, catch a glimpse of the sea from your bath, eat alfresco at The Lobster Shed. Unwind until you feel ready to head down the drive and rejoin the real world.

310 **THE TAWNY**

AT: CONSALL HALL
GARDENS ESTATE
Consall Lane
Consall,
Staffordshire
ST9 0AG
Central England
+44 (0)15 3878 7664
thetawny.co.uk

The Tawny has all the trappings of a luxury hotel stay, but it just looks a little different. Instead of one hotel building, it's a 70-acre estate with rooms and facilities dotted throughout the landscape, overlooking woodlands and lakes. The heart of the Tawny is the Plumicorn (found near reception, overlooking an outdoor heated swimming pool) where guests will find a restaurant and a bar. Bedrooms come in the form of huts, treehouses, boathouses and look-outs. They all have outdoor spa baths and peaceful private settings.

Sleepovers in
INCREDIBLE BUILDINGS

311 BUTLEY PRIORY

Woodbridge,
Suffolk
IP12 3NR
East of England
+44 (0)13 9445 0046
butleypriory.co.uk

Every corner of this 13th-century priory is dreamy. The huge Grade I-listed building, which sleeps thirteen, is all sweeping stone arches, huge fireplaces, medieval window seats and floaty fabrics in calming shades. The Priory is the former gatehouse to an Augustinian monastery, which was founded in 1171, and centuries ago welcomed royalty, even acting as a royal hunting lodge for a time. These days, the romantic building, surrounded by Suffolk woodland, is an otherworldly place you can call home for a few days.

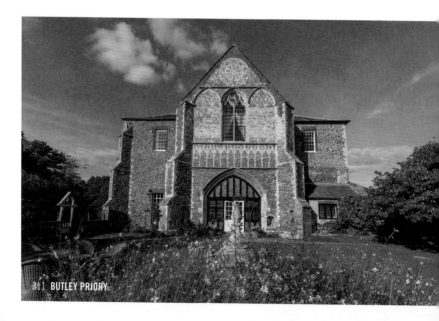

311 BUTLEY PRIORY

312 THE RUIN

AT: HACKFALL

Grewelthorpe,
North Yorkshire
HG4 3BS
North East
+44 (0)16 2882 5925
landmarktrust.org.uk

Sat at a high point with amazing views overlooking the landscape at Hackfall and beyond, The Ruin is one of the forest follies landowner William Aislabie created in the 18th century. While many of the woodland's other buildings have fallen into disrepair, The Ruin has a different story. It was saved by The Landmark Trust and turned into a holiday home that truly is one of a kind. The building has two identities – from the front it is Gothic in style while the side hidden from public view is rough and rugged, designed to evoke ancient Roman ruins. Uniquely, to access each of The Ruin's three rooms you must use the outside terrace. A nighttime trip to the bathroom has never felt more dramatic.

311 BUTLEY PRIORY

312 THE RUIN

313 EAST BANQUETING HOUSE

Chipping Campden,
Gloucestershire
GL55 6JE
South West
+44 (0)16 2882 5925
landmarktrust.org.uk

An incredible Jacobean building, flamboyant in design, with ornamental windows and chimneys, East Banqueting House was the height of architectural fashion when it was built in the early 17th century. Though, amazingly, it wasn't even the main attraction. Along with the West Banqueting House (which you can also rent), it stood on a grand terrace in the garden of Old Campden House. The main house was sadly destroyed during the Civil War by Royalists in 1645, but the estate's smaller buildings survived. The banqueting houses now stand alone in a field on the outskirts of Chipping Campden village; tiny time capsules – simply furnished so as to not distract from the incredible bones of the historic building – that make for a really atmospheric stay.

314 HOLE COTTAGE

Cowden,
Kent
TN8 5PD
South East
+44 (0)16 2882 5925
landmarktrust.org.uk

You can't help feeling like you've fallen back through time when you come across Hole Cottage in its quiet woodland clearing. Built during the late medieval period, top-heavy Hole Cottage is actually just one remaining section of what was once a grand, timber-framed hall house. Despite feeling like it's cut off from modern civilisation it is actually just a 15-minute walk to Cowden train station through the trees.

315 THE SUMMER FOLLY

AT: GRIMSTHORPE
CASTLE
Grimsthorpe,
Lincolnshire
PE10 0LY
Central England
+44 (0)16 3788 1183
uniquehome
stays.com

Tucked away in the grounds of Grimsthorpe Castle, this 18th-century folly was originally used as a summer house, a setting for picnics and parties (though it had an interesting spell hiding an anti-aircraft battery during WWII). It's now a whimsical holiday home, decorated with bold splashes of colour and hand-painted murals on the ceilings and walls. As well as access to a generous garden, guests are allowed to wander freely around the 3000 acres of the Grimsthorpe estate.

T R E E T O P *hideaways*

316 **HIVES**
AT: CALLOW HALL
Ashbourne
Derbyshire
DE6 2AA
Central England
+44 (0)13 3530 0900
wildhive.uk

Callow Hall is a country house hotel with an outdoorsy edge. In woodland beside the hotel you'll find a collection of Hives, little treehouses that are basically wooden hotel rooms out in the elements. Each timber clad Hive has a balcony with views of the leaves, Callow Hall's wild meadows and hills in the distance, plus everything you'd expect from the fanciest of hotel rooms: soft robes, lovely toiletries, a tiny kitchenette (complete with generous snack jar) and a cloud-like bed. Hive guests also benefit from all hotel facilities, like the Nordic sauna, treatment rooms, fire pit and complimentary bike rental. Buggies ferry you back and forth from the main hotel building if you don't fancy staggering back from dinner in the dark through the trees.

317 **LOST MEADOW TREEPOD**
AT: BROOM PARK FARM
Mount,
Cornwall
PL30 4DP
South West
+44 (0)11 7204 7830
wildishcornwall.co.uk

Fancy sleeping in a suspended wooden sphere? You can do just that on the edge of Bodmin Moor, where a small spherical bedroom hangs among the branches in a secluded stretch of woodland. On the ground below, you'll find a spring-fed shower, a composting loo and a field kitchen to whip up an alfresco brekkie. If that all sounds a tiny bit too off grid for you, there's a shipping container a few minutes' walk through the trees where you'll find charging points and a hair dryer.

318 THE POPPY TREEHOUSE

AT: FULLERTON FARM
Fullerton,
Hampshire
SP11 7LA
South East
+44 (0)11 7204 7830
canopyandstars.co.uk

Poppy sits at the end of a boardwalk, deep in woodland on the edge of Black Chalk Vineyard's neat rows of vines. Two outside terraces (one with a big tub) and enormous windows frame green views of the surrounding trees, while inside, Poppy feels like the treehouse of childhood imaginings, thanks to its cosy log burner and rustic going-on-an-adventure log cabin vibe.

319 THE BOWER TREEHOUSE

North Brewham,
Somerset
BA10 0JS
South West
+44 (0)11 7204 7830
canopyandstars.co.uk

Bower Treehouse is at the bottom of the owner's garden, but, down a windy path through woodland and facing out into rural Somerset countryside, you feel miles away from anyone else. With a roomy alfresco bath, woodburner, stack of board games, underfloor heating and a huge king-sized bed carved from oak, it's a dreamy mix of outdoorsy and luxurious. Sipping your morning cuppa on the deck, serenaded by birdsong and the trickle of a small stream flowing beneath the treehouse, you won't want to be anywhere else.

320 NYMETWOOD TREEHOUSES

Thorne Lane
Spreyton,
Devon
EX17 5AA
South West
+44 (0)78 7988 3939
nymetwood
treehouses.com

These two scandi-inspired treehouses, on a former farm now turned over to wildflower meadow, blend in seamlessly with their rural surroundings. Both are tucked in the tree canopy and made out of locally sourced, sustainable wood. Both boast stunning views of the Devon countryside from their glass-fronted bathrooms and living spaces – and from the huge copper baths on the deck outside. And the views don't stop there. Look skywards once you've climbed into bed to see stars twinkling and branches swaying overhead.

ISLAND *escapes*

321 LUNDY

Devon
South West
+44 (0)16 2882 5925
landmarktrust.org.uk

There's getting away from it all and then there's this kind of otherworldly isolation. Lundy is an island which sits off the north Devon coastline. Famous for its diverse landscape and wildlife populations (it's home to puffins, feral goats, grey seals, dolphins, whales and porpoises, to name a few), it's largely off-grid – there are no cars, phone signal is intermittent and electricity isn't available after midnight. But incredibly there are more than 20 places to stay the night on the island, each in unique buildings, like a former fisherman's cottage, the old lighthouse keeper's store (so small it sleeps just one) and what was once a Sunday school. There's also a shop and pub on the island, which is where visitors and island residents congregate, eat and can phone the mainland.

322 OSEA ISLAND

AT: BLACKWATER
ESTUARY
Essex
CM9 8UH
East of England
+44 (0)20 3026 4067
oseaisland.co.uk

Check-in and check-out time on Osea Island both depend on the tide times, as your route on and off the island is an ancient causeway built by the Romans which is only accessible for four hours at low tide. That's far from the only quirk about this privately owned tidal island, which is dotted with a collection of self-catering cottages, apartments and beach-side houses. It's all a little surreal, from the salt marshes and the Shack cinema to the incredible sense of seclusion.

323 FILLY ISLAND

South Cerney,
Gloucestershire
GL7 5TY
South West
+44 (0)16 3788 1183
uniquehome
stays.com

If you like the idea of an island, but don't fancy all out seclusion, this cottage, called Filly Island, is the answer. You can be the ruler of your very own tiny 'island', which is accessed by a humpback bridge, for a few nights here. The cute cottage is sat on a small triangular patch of land, between a millstream and the River Churn. It's in the heart of South Cerney village, so you're still firmly surrounded by civilization yet technically surrounded by water too. From Filly Island, a former cart-store which was built in the 1700s, at the tip of the triangle, you can embrace your watery location in comfort from your fancy terrace.

FARM STAYS

324 THE FARM AT AVEBURY

AT: GALTEEMORE FARM
Beckhampton,
near Avebury,
Wiltshire
SN8 1FE
South West
+44 (0)77 9002 6363
thefarmat
avebury.co.uk

A handful of converted stables, all set around a pretty communal courtyard, The Farm at Avebury is a little (and much less muddy) part of a real working farm that you're encouraged to explore during your stay. Take a short walk from your stable and you'll come face to face with horses, cows and pigs. Wander a little further and you'll see the huge hump of Silbury Hill. Each of the stables has been kitted out in bold and aesthetically pleasing interiors that are a joy to return to after a day in the countryside.

325 DROVERS' BOUGH

Lower Maescoed,
Herefordshire
HR2 0HP
Central England
+44 (0)11 7204 7830
+44 (0)19 8151 0548
droversbough.com

Set on Gwyrlodydd farm in the foothills of the Black Mountains, Drovers' Bough is a tall cabin on stilts hidden among the 27 acres of self-sufficient farmland. It's positioned over an ancient drovers track (a route for moving large herds of livestock from one place to another), up high so animals could, in theory, still pass underneath. You can keep yourself to yourself, with only birdsong for company, or explore the farm to spot goats, rare breed bantams, peacocks, geese, guinea fowl and an emu called Joni.

326 GLEBE HOUSE

Southleigh,
Devon
EX24 6SD
South West
+44 (0)14 0487 1276
glebehousedevon.co.uk

A stay at Glebe House is as much about the food as it is about the rooms, which are so richly and creatively decorated you'll spend your journey home mentally redesigning your own house. (The Rose Room and The Old Kitchen are especially lovely, while the communal living space and airy garden room are the stuff design dreams are made of.) A 15-acre smallholding and self-styled *agroturismo*, Glebe House sits at the top of a steep hill overlooking a patchwork of farmland and forest. At the weekend, it's also a dining destination for guests and locals. The clever five-part menu changes daily, depending on what's ripened in the farm's polytunnel or been dug up in the kitchen garden. They also keep pigs which you can visit on a wander around the grounds – if you don't get distracted by the heated pool or the tennis courts first, that is.

Concealed **CABINS**

---

327 **THE ROOST**

*AT: ELMLEY NATURE
RESERVE*

*Isle of Sheppey,
Kent
ME12 3RW
South East
+44 (0)17 9566 4896
elmleynature
reserve.co.uk*

This is the only nature reserve in England where you can stay the night – and you catch your 40 winks in serious comfort too. In secluded spots, surrounded by flat swathes of grassland and coastal marshes that stretch out towards the sea, you'll find a handful of homely cabins and shepherd's huts. The Roost has big views from the bed – and the outdoor tub – of Elmley's unique wetland landscape. You might even get some birdwatching in from beneath the bubbles.

328 **WOOD CABIN**

AT: SWALLOWTAIL HILL

*Hobbs Lane
Beckley,
East Sussex
TN31 6TT
South East
+44 (0)17 9726 0890
swallowtailhill.com*

Down a bumpy farm track at the bottom of a hill, Wood Cabin sits a little way off from its neighbour Penfold Cabin. Both are wonderfully rustic, off-grid creations. Each comes with a fire pit, a compost toilet and a gloriously hot outdoor shower with lush views over the meadow. There's also an undercover dining and kitchen prep area with coolboxes, where you'll find pots and pans to heat up your pre-ordered hearty stews or BBQ over the flames. Thankfully, there are lanterns provided to help you navigate to the loo in the middle of the night, but otherwise it's just you, the fire and the twinkly night sky.

329 LARK

AT: A PLACE
IN THE PINES
Thimbleby,
North Yorkshire
DL6 3PY
North East
+44 (0)75 9055 8986
aplaceinthe
pines.co.uk

Lark is on the edge of the North York Moors National Park. A rural Scandi-style cabin – all sleek wooden shapes and simple interiors – encircled by trees. Outside you'll find a fire pit, a pretty pond, a bathing deck complete with two outdoor baths and a woodland, which you have free reign of during your stay. If you need a pause from the wholesome, outdoorsy vibes, the local pub is only a 10-minute walk away.

330 HINTERLANDES CABIN

Secret location
Cumbria
North West
+44 (0)11 7204 7830
canopyandstars.co.uk

A stay so hidden that you won't even know the exact address until a short time before you arrive. Hinterlandes Cabin moves location every 28 days. The cabin is totally off-grid and self-sufficient so leaves no footprint on the land it borrows. Great views and access to incredible, lesser-visited parts of the Lake District are guaranteed. You can also be sure you'll have zero Wi-Fi and little phone signal, though the wood burner, wood-fired hot tub, books and games should more than make up for that.

331 KITTYLANDS

AT: ALLER DORSET
Aller Lane
Lower Ansty,
Dorset
DT2 7PX
South West
+44 (0)12 5888 0696
allerdorset.com

Aller Farm is home to four little cabins with big personalities. Two (Links and Littledown) are shepherd's huts but not as you know them – these are boldly decorated, bougie huts with huge windows. The mega interiors continue into cabins Zoulands and Kittylands. With bright pink and green accents, plush indoor *and* outdoor bathrooms (the alfresco one is tiled with a double-ended roll top bath), a firepit and a log burner for chilly nights, Kittylands is the kind of cabin you could happily curl up in for an entire season.

332 **THE BIDE**

Milton Road
Milton Meadow,
Dorset
DT11 0DP
South West
thebide.com

A big red box in the leafy corner of a Dorset field, The Bide probably isn't what initially springs to mind when you think cabin. It's an unusual design and shape, all clad in corrugated, rust-coloured corrapol. Owners Caroline and Scott have favoured sustainability while designing and building the hideaway – insulation is provided by sheeps wool, and the bathroom features a sleek compost loo and a vaporising shower which is cleverly designed to use less water. Check out the wood-fired hot tub on the deck, with views of the surrounding farmland, or, if the weather is less favourable, soak it all up from inside before drawing the blinds and setting up the in-cabin projector cinema.

CASTLES *you can kip in*

333 KINGSWEAR CASTLE

Kingswear,
Devon
TQ6 oDX
South West
+44 (0)16 2882 5925
landmarktrust.org.uk

An entire 16th-century castle, perched on the rocks opposite Dartmouth, can be yours for a weekend. It's not huge – it sleeps four in two bedrooms – but it feels mighty. Kingswear is all chunky walls, ancient stone floors and proper battlements, sat right on the edge of the surf with unrivalled views out to sea. Completed in 1502, Kingswear Castle was once designed to defend the harbour, but now it's a special setting for a whiling away peaceful hours. The best spot is the roof terrace, where you can watch boats and wildlife bob past, and raise and lower your very own flag.

334 BAMBURGH CASTLE

Bamburgh,
Northumberland
NE69 7DF
North East
+44 (0)16 6821 4208
bamburghcastle.com

Beautiful Bamburgh Castle has stood overlooking the Northumberland coastline for more than 1400 years. Huge and impressive, it's seen conflict and prosperity. It's been a hospital, a coastguard station, a home to royalty and left to ruin – and it's now the private home of the Armstrong family. Thousands visit the castle each year but only a lucky few get to wake up here. The 13th-century Clock Tower, which is built into the castle walls, is available as unique accommodation, with epic views of the castle itself and of Bamburgh beach, plus after-hours access to the castle grounds.

335 BLENCOWE HALL

AT: THE ROWLEY
ESTATES
Blencowe,
Cumbria
CA11 0DF
North West
+44 (0)79 6825 8234
therowleyestates.com

Old meets new at Blencowe Hall, a 14th-century castle which has won awards for its unique restoration. A few years ago, the entire Grade I-listed hall was on the 'at risk' register. Its towers were roofless, and there was a large V-shaped split in one of them, thanks to cannon fire during the Civil War. When it was restored, that gaping hole was stabilised and retained, the space stitched together with glass and balconies that fill the historic building with light. It's now a plush holiday home sleeping 24 that seamlessly blends history with modern comforts.

336 ASTLEY CASTLE

Church Lane
Astley,
Warwickshire
CV10 7QN
Central England
+44 (0)16 2882 5925
landmarktrust.org.uk

Here's another clever update to a historic castle. 12th-century Astley Castle – a fine example of a fortified manor, complete with moat and grand gateway – has had an interesting history. It passed down through the Grey family during the Tudor period, during which time three Grey women became queen, including Lady Jane Grey who famously was queen for just nine days. Astley Castle became a ruin in 1978 after being gutted by a fire, but The Landmark Trust restored it in 2005, cleverly creating modern accommodation within the historic ruins. What could be saved has been, and sensitively blended with new interiors. Imagine open plan living surrounded by ancient stone and floor-to-ceiling windows framing ruins that couldn't be saved. It makes for a magical place to stay.

ARCHITECTURAL *abodes*

337 BALANCING BARN

Thorington,
Suffolk
IP19 9JG
East of England
+44 (0)20 3488 1584
living-
architecture.co.uk

Two things are unusual about architect-designed Balancing Barn. The 30-metre-long house is completely clad in reflective steel tiles, creating a mirrored effect so the building almost blends into its surroundings. Half of it is also suspended over the edge of a hillside. Nowhere is its cantilevered design more apparent than in the living room, where big windows and a glass floor are a constant reminder that you're suspended in space. Just to really cement that playful feel, guests will also find a swing underneath the house.

338 A HOUSE FOR ESSEX

Black Boy Lane
Wrabness,
Essex
CO11 2TP
East of England
+44 (0)20 3488 1584
living-
architecture.co.uk

Designed by artist Grayson Perry and FAT Architecture, A House for Essex is an artwork in its own right. Colourful and eccentric, decorative and ornamental, it's inspired by chapels and roadside memorials, and is supposed to be a tribute to the county of Essex and to Julie Cope, a fictional every-woman of Essex created by Perry. The result is a house like no other, covered in glazed tiles with rooftop sculptures, and decorated with bespoke artworks and mosaics. It's available for two- or three-night stays.

339 KUDHVA

Sanding Road
Trebarwith Strand,
Cornwall
PL34 0HH
South West
kudhva.com

There's camping and then there's this: sleeping in an abandoned quarry in an off-grid pod on stilts. Kudhvas are unusual-looking, design-led cabins raised off the ground with big views of their rural, coastal surroundings. The facilities are basic, but that's kind of the point. There are USB chargers and solar-powered showers at reception, but you could just let your phone run out of battery and spend your stay foraging, surfing and swimming in the on-site reservoir, then making new pals at the communal kitchen.

WATERSIDE *homes*

340 **SHINGLE HOUSE**

Dungeness Road
Dungeness,
Kent
TN29 9NE
South East
+44 (0)20 3488 1584
living-
architecture.co.uk

You can really immerse yourself in the surreal vibe of Dungeness at Shingle House, where expansive windows flood the house with coastal light and frame views of wild flower-studded shingle and the sea beyond (as well as the Romney, Hythe & Dymchurch miniature railway, which passes by the end of the garden.) Shingle House is an architectural take on Dungeness's simple, tarred fisherman shacks, which continue to define the landscape.

340 SHINGLE HOUSE

341 CABÜ BY THE SEA

Dymchurch Road
St Mary's Bay,
Kent
TN29 0HF
South East
+44 (0)13 0366 9033
holidays.cabu.co.uk

CABÜ's timber cabins are design-led creations on the shingle near Dungeness in Kent. The cabins come in varying shapes and sizes but all have floor-to-ceiling windows, BBQ decks and incredibly photogenic interiors. They sit on a private patch of land just behind the sea wall, mere steps from the beach, but clustered around a heated swimming pool too (with hot tubs and saunas nearby) if the English Channel's waves are a little too chilly. You can make friends over the communal griddle tables at the Sitooterie if you like, or stick to the privacy of your own patch. Don't miss Cabü Corner, a shop where you can stock up on holiday 'essentials' like retro sweets, kites, fancy coffee and big bottles of Aperol.

342 THE RAFT AT CHIGBOROUGH

AT: CHIGBOROUGH
FARM
Heybridge,
Essex
CM9 4RE
East of England
+44 (0)11 7204 7830
canopyandstars.co.uk

You're not just sleeping near the water here, you're literally floating on it. The Raft is a cabin which is afloat on its own private lake. Load up a wheelbarrow with your bags and you can reach the cabin, which is around 30 metres from the bank, chain ferry style. Once on board you'll discover a two-storey, solar-powered log cabin complete with BBQ, alfresco hot shower, binoculars for bird-watching and a telescope for star-gazing. The owners don't recommend swimming in the lake, but they do provide a rowing boat for exploring the water. You could even row over to the wood-fired hot tub, which is on the edge of the lake, for a long, soothing soak.

343 THE SIGNAL STATION

Lloyds Road
Lizard,
Cornwall
TR12 7AP
South West
+44 (0)16 3788 1183
uniquehome
stays.com

Built in 1872, Lloyd's Signal Station, which sits high on the clifftops of the Lizard Peninsula, was designed to be a communication hub for passing ships. Flag signals were used from the tower to direct trading vessels, while information about outward- and homeward-bound boats was passed onto London via telegraph. The lookout ceased operations in the 1960s and is now a remote holiday home. From your unique stance at England's most southerly point, you can enjoy views of the coastline – stunning whether it's stormy or still – from pretty much every single window, as well as from your incredible roof terrace.

Picturebook COTTAGES

344 BRIDGE COTTAGE

Peppercombe,
near Bideford,
Devon
EX39 5QD
South West
+44 (0)16 2882 5925
landmarktrust.org.uk

Painted inside and out in pleasing, soft shades of pink and green, thatched Bridge Cottage is one pretty cottage. It dates from around 1820, and is beside the path that leads steeply downhill through a wooded valley to Peppercombe Beach. Tranquility is yours in this sleepy part of Devon, and you're almost guaranteed to have the pebbly beach to yourself.

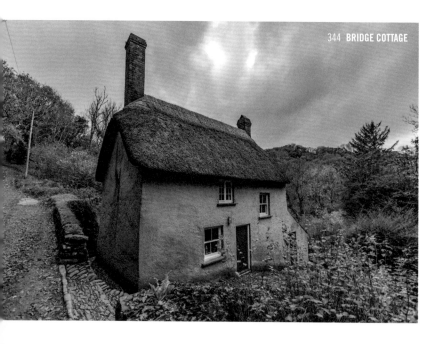

344 BRIDGE COTTAGE

345 PEAK DISTRICT BARN

Alstonefield,
Staffordshire
DE6 2FX
Central England
kiphideaways.com

Pulling up outside picture-perfect Peak District Barn feels like a real treat. The cottage, one of Kip Hideaways' handpicked collection, is a neat stone building with a pretty garden and pastel-painted front door. Inside the layout is flipped; two plush bedrooms are found on the ground floor which means dreamy views of the village of Alstonefield and the Peaks in the distance from your open-plan living room kitchen. It's a soothing space to return to with weary feet at the end of the day. Light the log burner and curl up with a cuppa in a window seat (or the rocking chair, or the big freestanding bath) for the evening.

346 COVE COTTAGE

Main Road
West Lulworth,
Dorset
BH20 5RQ
South West
+44 (0)19 2940 0888
lulworth.com

Cove Cottage, a neat thatched cottage on the path down to Lulworth Cove, is postcard pretty. The *orné*-style cottage is simple yet decorative, with delicate windows and symmetrical pastel-painted doors. Inside, the delights continue with thoughtfully picked furniture and fabrics, and more quirky period features. It couldn't be in a nicer setting either, walking distance to both Lulworth Cove and Durdle Door, the stars of England's UNESCO Jurassic Coast.

347 BUSH COTTAGE

Chorley,
Shropshire
WV16 6PR
Central England
+44 (0)16 2882 5925
landmarktrust.org.uk

A petite two-up-two-down cottage, this place is everything an English country cottage should be. Red brick and oak, with a little chimney and pretty lattice windows. There are even actual roses around the door. You'll find Bush Cottage off a rural track, sitting alone in a lush Shropshire valley where it's been watching the seasons change since 1548.

348 ROSE CASTLE COTTAGE

Tarn Hows,
Cumbria
LA22 8AQ
North West
+44 (0)34 4800 2070
nationaltrust.org.uk

If the snow-covered cottage from festive film *The Holiday* is what springs to mind when you think of an English cottage, this two-bedroom delight will not disappoint. Built out of local stone with symmetrical white arched windows, Rose Castle Cottage is sat just above Tarn Hows lake, and has heaps of historical character. Access is down a narrow track and you'll be all alone in the countryside here, with no neighbours to be found. The cottage isn't quite in the 21st century. It's heated by the wood-fired log burner while electricity comes from batteries, so you can charge your phone but nothing else. You won't find a TV or even Wi-Fi here either, but the rural Lake District views out of the window should be enough to keep you entertained.

349 HEX COTTAGE

AT: SIBTON ESTATE
Yoxford Road
Sibton,
Suffolk
IP17 2LZ
East of England
+44 (0)19 8680 2113
wilderness
reserve.com

Describing thatched Hex Cottage as charming does it a disservice. The tiny secluded cottage is mesmerising. It's also entirely off-grid, which means zero electricity – it's heated by a wood-burning range and at night, it's lit by the flicker of fire and candlelight. Off-grid doesn't mean compromising on comfort though. You'll find a huge bed and roll top bath, plus plenty of books (look out for witchy-themes that live up to the cottage's name) and games to keep you entertained as the light fades. You also get access to Sibton Estate's facilities nearby, which include a swimming pool and hot tub, plus bike and rowing boat hire. But you might just find you want to stay put in your own little fairytale.

INDEX

COLOPHON

EDITING *and* COMPOSING — Ellie Walker-Arnott
GRAPHIC DESIGN — Joke Gossé and doublebill.design
PHOTOGRAPHY — Sam Mellish — sammellish.com
COVER IMAGE — The Minack Theatre (secret 28)

The addresses in this book have been selected after thorough independent research by the author, in collaboration with Luster Publishing. The selection is solely based on personal evaluation of the business by the author. Nothing in this book was published in exchange for payment or benefits of any kind.

D/2023/12.005/10
ISBN 978 94 6058 3384
NUR 510, 512

© 2023 Luster Publishing, Antwerp
First edition, May 2023
lusterpublishing.com — THE500HIDDENSECRETS.COM
info@lusterpublishing.com

Printed in Italy by Printer Trento.

MIX
Paper | Supporting responsible forestry
FSC® C015829